BE A SPIDER, BUILD A WEB

STICKY CONTENT MARKETING FOR SMALL BUSINESSES

RACHEL KLAVER

SPUD HOUSE PUBLISHING

Published by Spud House Publishing

Website: beaspiderbuildaweb.com

A catalogue record for this book is available from the National Library of New Zealand.

ISBN 978-0-473-62646-4 (paperback)

ISBN 978-0-473-62648-8 (EPUB)

Credits: Illustrations by Rebekah Potter. Editor: Susie Klaver.

CONTENTS

PART SIX
THE RADIUS LINES

PART SEVEN
THE CAPTURE SPIRAL

PART EIGHT
TROUBLESHOOTING

PART NINE
OVER TO YOU NOW

PREFACE

Hey there.

You're about to read my take on content marketing (or listen to it.) Before we start building your web, I wanted to say a huge thank you. Thank you for entrusting me with your time. I'm a busy business owner like you, and I know carving out learning time is a big deal.

Thank you also for being brave to pick up a book about being a spider. I know that might have felt uncomfortable. I promise there aren't close-up spider pics littered through the book. You're safe.

MARKETING IS NOT A JOURNEY OF STRAIGHT LINES

I'm going to teach you how to think like a spider building a web.

But to do that, we have got to jump around a little. That's because marketing is not a straight line. You can't do just one action. It will always lead to another action, and then another action, because human beings are complicated and they don't always do exactly what we want. (Life would be so much easier if they did, but creativity and surprise and innovation would disappear.)

Think of it like trying to get a two-year-old to do the same thing, every morning without fail. One day they will do it, but the next day you can almost guarantee they will deny ever knowing how to do it.

For anyone who has tried to cut toast for a toddler—one day they will only eat them in triangles, and so the next day you do triangles again, and they won't eat them because that was yesterday and today it's only about square toast.

You can't pre-empt the mind of a toddler. This can be incredibly frustrating. To this day I have never experienced the levels of rage I felt trying to convince a completely unreasonable toddler that SQUARE TOAST TASTES THE SAME AS TRIANGLE TOAST!

We're going to talk about toddler and adult minds later in this book, and why it's important to understand them when it comes to marketing and building a content web. However, one thing I've learned is no matter how old we are, we don't all think, or act the same. We all take different pathways to get to a destination and it's not our job as business owners and marketers to decide the specific route, timing and intensity of the trip a new customer takes to our door.

We are going to create a content marketing web that gives your business the opportunity to have lots of different touch points (ways for people to find out about you) while building trust in your business. It will help them to work out you're the right person for them, so that they then come and choose you!

Marketing is making a web. It's why I don't like the word funnel— because funnels relate to an orderly process. It gives us this image of shoving a bunch of people at the top of a slippery slope, with a number of them popping out the bottom as customers.

Be prepared that this book may jump around the web a little, because human behaviour is not linear. As we move through the book, you'll understand why that is.

(The downloadable PDF that goes with this book will help. Print it out before you begin as it will assist with the marketing web you create as you move through the book. It helps you put all the information into the correct order! You can get it from **beaspiderbuildaweb.com.**)

INTRODUCTION

A LITTLE BIT ABOUT ME AND THIS BOOK

I thought it would be a good idea to introduce you to… me!

If you already know who I am, feel free to skip it over. And while I know these things can seem a little bit self-indulgent, I want to talk to you a little bit about who I am and how I got into marketing.

I am a person who, just like you, is a business owner who had to learn how to market myself and my business to survive. First when I was a single parent raising three kids and trying to make sure I had enough work coming through on a regular basis as a freelance writer, and later as a trainer and a facilitator. In these situations, I had to find ways to market my business effectively on a very small budget.

I got into social media and digital marketing pretty early on. I first learned to write copy when websites were basically long letters, and no images. All the important sentences highlighted in yellow, and garish lime green call to action buttons everywhere. I blogged to feel more connected to the world, and I used social media to find my people, build a community for myself, and later, make money.

I became a full-time freelance writer after starting a family, working when they slept. Over eight years I managed to write hundreds of articles for publications around the world, along with twenty-seven books, mostly in the educational field. My career highlight was the week I had articles across seven magazines in the supermarket rack, some under a pseudonym because my name was just too saturated. My biggest win was reselling an article I had written for a magazine in New Zealand into other publications around the world, making around five thousand dollars for it overall. Not bad for one 1500-word article! Now that's near impossible, with so many publications publishing online. Even then I was learning the power of repurposing.

I used social media to connect with people outside my little farmhouse. I knew social media was going to be huge for businesses. As I became noticed online, I got asked to go into ad agencies, PR and marketing companies to help explain to the team why they should be offering social media marketing options to their clients. Some listened, others thought I was crazy, and the fad of social media would die out.

As we all know, those guys were wrong.

I was an influencer before they were cool. I spent a few years getting paid in makeup, sneakers, glasses, free tickets, and clothes. It looked glamorous until I had to use my gifted shampoo to wash my (free) clothes because I couldn't afford washing powder!

I moved from my business working with parents and teachers, into marketing training. To be honest, it was mainly to have more child friendly hours and stay home more. But marketing and I were finally able to move into a committed relationship together!

Then, as we grew our own marketing agency and launched that, I had to learn again how to make marketing fit in with an increasingly busy life, including managing a team and working out how to make sure our current clients are happy. And you know what? Some of that I failed miserably at.

Today, I own our company Identify with my husband Rod and we are really lucky in that some of our children also work with us part time alongside study. We also have an amazing team of other marketers to help us serve our clients.

Here's why we 'do what we do'. So many business owners find marketing terrifying. Many marketers fill heads with jargon that's tricky to understand. There's so many things to remember—like the four Ps and other models that are seen as essential marketing tools. I'm not that great at retaining information when it is in that textbook format. I do understand marketing models, however I always feel anxious when I'm around a trained marketer, because if they start talking about those things from the 'textbook', I panic. What's funny though, is that I am actually using those models in practice—I just don't know the special name for them!

You won't see a lot of technical language in this book. Instead it's practical know-how and making things as simple as possible. I'm not dumbing marketing down. It's just that technical information can confuse the issue and makes us all feel a bit more nervous than we need to be.

Our mission is to help every small business owner understand marketing better and feel more confident in doing their own marketing, or outsourcing when they are ready. That's what this book is for.

PART ONE
THE SPIDER AND THE WEB

CHAPTER 1

WHY YOU NEED TO BE A SPIDER

I think in pictures and stories. It helps me understand a concept and tie it to something I understand. My brain is either going at six hundred kilometres an hour or desperately empty, and the way I file my ideas in my brain is similar to the desk situation I've got, where ideas and concepts are layered in piles around me.

I need a story to help link the ideas in my head. And thankfully the story of spiders and their webs helps me understand the intricacies of marketing better than anything else I've found.

I'm fascinated by the beauty that spiders can create, as they spin a web that will capture their prey.

I want you to be a marketing spider, and build a web to draw people in.

I'm pretty sure the marketing web I'm building with this book won't attract arachnophobes to it. I do understand that for many the thought of being a spider is akin to asking you to listen to fingernails down a blackboard on repeat (shudder), and if that's you, there's a content warning for this chapter—we're talking spiders and webs.

I promise you, it will get easier after this chapter!

DON'T BE A NASTY SPIDER

Sales and marketing can get a lot of stick sometimes and, to be honest, some of it's fair. People use half truths and fakery to paint a picture of who they are, and what their business does to sell a story of possibilities.

Our brains love stories of triumph. We want stories that make us feel we can do it too. We love the pull to the big idea, we all want a promise of easy wins.

Sometimes those stories get a little over the top, and a story can slide from showing your best side to showing your imaginary side. It skimps far too much on reality, and makes promises it can't keep

When I first started marketing, I used to use the term "smoke and mirrors". My first team member at Identify used to tell me we had to pretend to be bigger than we were to get clients, to fake it until we made it.

It's a little like solopreneurs putting "we" all over their websites to pretend that the business is operated and run by more than them. Changing from "I" to "we" once you've grown is an easy fix, but before then, there's no shame in being a 'you' In fact, many prefer working with an "I" over a "we". (I talk a little more on this in Chapter 17)

It no longer sits well with me to pretend to be more than we are. I think our customers deserve to see the real us, and make a choice based on that. When I'm speaking with our community, I'm focussed on telling them what we're really doing, as opposed to what looks perfect.

A nasty spider spends thousands on a spectacular neon web that promises transformation with a click, but then only gives out a passable product when you sign over your money.

Don't be that type of nasty spider.

Nasty spiders are also keen hunters. They sit on their webs, with their eagle eyes out for any disturbance that heralds a new follower, a new connection, a visitor to their website. They want to POUNCE and seize the first available moment to convert their new contact to a new customer.

NO ONE LIKES BEING SPIED ON

The chat on our website is connected to our CRM (our client relationship management system where we store our information about clients and "almost" clients). I used to love popping on and watching it track people coming and going.

Most of them were unnamed strangers, but every now and again it would let me know someone from our list was on our site.

Just after completing a sales call with a business owner, I noticed she'd popped back onto the website. Yes! It looked like she was super keen, and was checking us out.

I decided to say hi to her via chat.

It did not go down well. She totally freaked out about my "stalking" behaviour, told me the deal was off, and to wipe her off our database forever.

I was being a nasty spider.

Using site tracking can also go really well. The trick is to not jump too fast. About a week after this incident, I noticed a client was popping onto our website every day. As we hadn't done any work with him for over a year, I dropped him a note.

It went a little like this:

"Hi there (name)

For some reason (heh, we know the reason!), you've been in my thoughts, and I thought I'd check how you are going. How's business?

Regards

Rachel.

Within five minutes I got a reply.

Rachel!

What WITCHCRAFT is this? I've been planning to email you. I've got some more work to do with you, can we set up a meeting?"

We had a meeting, and I made a fairly big sale from a cheeky email.

Sometimes it's ok to give someone a "kind spider" nudge. We just don't want to jump on them with our fangs ready to bite!

THEY CAN SMELL DESPERATION

If sales are pouring in, and you're at capacity, it's easy to feel relaxed about selling.

It's harder when the phone hasn't rung in two weeks, the courier can't remember your address anymore and the bank balance is shrinking at an alarming rate.

The key is to hold the opportunity of a sale lightly in your hand. It's our job to serve, to listen to needs, show our best side in meeting those needs, and follow up as we've promised until the person says no.

It's not our job to push, make demands, and berate someone for not choosing us.

I've been hurt by the rejection of a prospect who has chosen someone else over me when I really wanted their business.

Sales is so much like dating. Sometimes one person is more enamoured than the other, and sometimes that person will be you as the business owner.

The relationship works best when the feeling is mutual and you can't force that. It just is.

Several years ago I had a regular collection of clients coming to me after going through a sales process with a competitor. This guy was what I'd term a nasty spider. He'd pounce, love bomb them with promises and attention, and then expected they'd convert

If they said no, he'd leave them nasty messages on Facebook, send copious emotional emails, and try to manipulate them into saying yes.

If we're having to push what we do onto others, we'll only serve to push them away. No one wants to do business with a nasty spider.

WE ARE KIND SPIDERS

You and me, we are not nasty spiders.

We're kind. We are super relaxed.

We trust the process, We trust our potential clients to make good decisions

Good decisions that include working with us, or buying our products.

We know who we are targeting.

We know what our offer is.

We know our core message.

And we know where our target people hang out.

We're going to spin a sticky web that our kind of people like.

And then we're going to sit, wait, and let them come to us in their own time.

As they arrive on our web we'll be friendly.

If they talk to us we'll talk back.

We'll show them we care with no strings.

And we'll let them find us in the places they like to hang out.

We'll give them the opportunity to come a little closer, and make it as easy as possible for them to do so, but if they aren't ready we'll accept it and stay friendly.

We're kind spiders.

We've got no desire to wrap them up in our spidy silk, inject them with our poison, and suck all the goodness out of them once they're liquified.

We want them energised, happy, and free to leave, so they can come back with others, or come back for themselves.

We're kind spiders.

Repeat after me

WE ARE KIND SPIDERS.

I WOULDN'T WANT TO BE A FLY

Besides one particular type of spider who just likes to wrap their trapped prey up in spidery silk so tight they essentially suffocate (sorry arachnophobes!), most spiders tend to use their sticky web to catch their prey, run out to them, and give them a liquifying poison that turns their insides to mush, allowing the spider to suck all the goodness out.

Essentially that spider turns their dinner into a juicy protein shake.

(I do hope you're not reading this just before turning the lights out!)

So when I tell you I want you to be a spider and build a web, I'm asking you to be a kind spider. The non- killing sort. I still want you to be fed of course, but we're not going to need to kill anything to make that happen. I promise!

Here's how you're going to be like a spider:

1. You're going to create a strong web spun with threads made of trust.
2. You're going to make your web attractive, and sticky so people are drawn to it, and hang around on it.
3. You're going to be patient and let people come to the Hub of the web in their time.
4. You're going to be ready to close the sale.

5. You're going to make sure you look after them, and keep on feeding them up, so they're happy.
6. You're going to let them keep hanging out with you on that web, and make it such a cool place to hang that they want their mates to come hang with them.

By the way, when researching for this book, I discovered that the average house has between sixty-one and sixty-two spiders in it. That's approximately fifty-six more than I would have guessed!

I PREFER WEBS OVER FUNNELS

A lot of marketers talk about creating funnels.

We also use the word funnel when we're helping a client create a structure for digital advertising.

Marketers love talking funnels because funnels are measurable. They help us create reports that show conversion rates, and the different what you can expect at each step.

I'm not anti numbers. We need them to check our marketing is working, and the time and effort we're putting in is making a difference.

I am anti making all our marketing activity revolve around building out funnels.

Funnels do not accurately describe how someone comes to us to work with us because the path is rarely smooth, logical or linear. Us humans are super annoying like that!

Here's is a picture of a funnel.

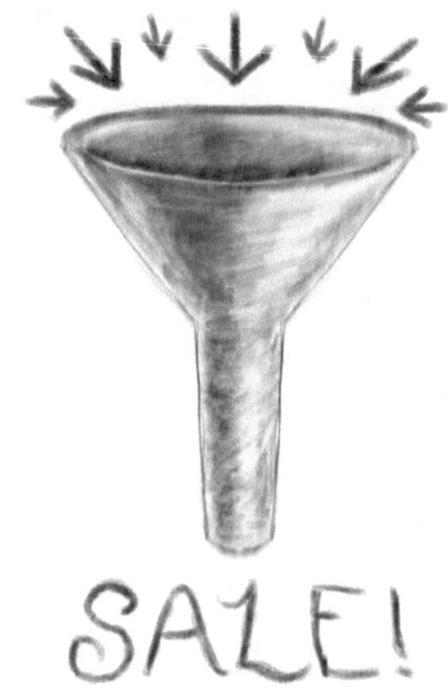

The basic idea of a funnel is that you pop people in at the top, and they slide down the side, collecting extra points of engagement score! The steps often look a bit like this:

They followed you.

They commented on a post!

They sent you a private message.

They gave you an email address in exchange for a free download.

They bought a cheap offer and are reading your carefully drafted emails.

They make a time or buy the big things.

and then BOOM they're now a client!

The closer they get to becoming a client, the more people drop off. Taking a look at the funnel shape, I'm not entirely sure how they escape. Are there secret trapdoors in the funnel no one talks about where the disinterested and disheartened can sneak out?

I'm not sure. But it is a numbers game.

You could have a hundred people come into that funnel, and by the time we get to the "commenting on a post" stage, you've already lost thirty percent.

Down the numbers drop, with a good estimate of somewhere between one to four out of that one hundred people becoming a client or purchasing from you.

But I'm still here wondering where all those other people are. The ones who didn't manage to squeeze themselves through that tiny little tube at the bottom of the funnel and escape. Where are they?

We're not going to build funnels. We're going to build a web.

CHAPTER 2

THE ANATOMY OF A SPIDER'S WEB

WHEN I STARTED TO FIND WAYS TO EXPLAIN MARKETING CONCEPTS IN A way that people could understand and remember, I often tied them to other things I already knew a little about.

A lot of the stories and analogies in this book are me doing exactly this. The most consistent one of all was "Be a Spider, Build a Web".

My clients, and people who've heard me speak will reference it in their own posts or use the phrase to help them plan their own marketing.

This book's title was born out of a night of dissatisfaction about what I was writing. I was three quarters of the way through writing this book, finding it tricky to motivate myself to complete it, and bothered with my original concept. So I got up in the very early morning, and I slashed away at my book, and made a change. I destroyed the web I was building to make another that is more deeply anchored in who I am, what I teach, and my own voice.

Several hours later I realised I should really learn a little more about spider's webs. For us to understand marketing as a spider, we need to understand a spider's web.

SPIDERS MAKE INTRICATE WEBS

When I was eight, our teacher did an art activity I've never forgotten. I'd never recommend anyone do it now. It seems pretty damaging to a spider's environment, so I'm sure it's not allowed anymore.

We'd go spiderweb hunting in the early morning, while the web was still wet with dew. We'd go out and shake talcum powder all over the web, and then press a piece of black paper that had been sprayed with hairspray onto it.

The spider's web would then come away onto the paper and dry. We called it a print, but really we were stealing that spider's artwork and glueing it onto paper with some rather strong smelling hairspray (they don't make it like they used to!)

While now I see I was robbing a spider of their home, back then I was too busy being captivated by the intricacy of the spider's work. So much time was taken in creating this incredible feat of design.

HOW THE WEB IS MADE

Webs come in all shapes and sizes, and some created in a slightly different way but for this, I want you to imagine a web made by a garden spider.

Here's an image of a garden spider's web:

Their webs require a lot of patience, and objects to catch on.

The spider starts by finding a strong anchor point. They attach their silk to it, and spin an anchor thread to another stable surface.

They pull this thread tight to make it strong, then spin a bridging thread to another strong surface then travel back down to the anchor, pulling in each line so there is a strong triangle shape.

From there, the spider drops down to the centre of the triangle, releases their spider silk and lets the wind catch the thread. It lands on an anchor or bridge thread, and then is pulled tight. This is the first radius of the web.

The spider repeats this up to twenty times, creating radius lines from the same centre, adding a few double threads to strengthen key lines, or to help frame the web tidily.

Once the lines are all out, the spider checks which lines will best withstand all weathers and unexpected events. Some of the radius lines will be cut, leaving the strongest.

It's now time to make the capture spiral. Starting at the furthest point of the centre, the spider weaves their web, dropping their silk around in an ever-decreasing spiral. The closer the spider comes into the centre, the closer the lines become, and the sticker the web.

Every now and again, the spider does a U-turn in the web, and backtracks to ensure the web lines are strong, especially around the outer edges of the web's spiral.

Once completed, the spider moves to the middle of the web, which is called the Hub. This is where they wait patiently for visitors to their web.

The end result of their hard work is a beautiful and intricate design. Just like your content web will become.

THE ELEMENTS OF A WEB FOR YOUR BUSINESS

In this book we'll be using some of the spidery terms for web making for our content. This has two benefits:

1. You get to understand content marketing with concepts without loads of marketing jargon, which hopefully makes it more memorable
2. I can feel COMPLETELY justified in calling this book *Be a Spider, Build a Web*.

The Anchor Point

Your anchor point needs to be a solid foundation. For you as a business, this is your values, your target market, and your pricing.

If the anchor is connected to unstable ground, the entire integrity of the web is compromised. You can still spin a web, but it's unlikely to be strong enough to capture and keep all the people you're going to want to attract.

You'll spend more time trying to fix issues in your business than being able to rest and allow the web to do its thing.

Spending time finding the anchor point is hard work, but it's key to being a clever spider.

The Bridge Thread

Your bridge thread allows your web to take shape. It's the core messaging that ties everything together, and allows you to spin your content. It helps amplify the stability of the anchor point.

The Radius

In a spider's web these are the spokes that come out from the centre. In your marketing, each one of these represents a different platform for your content marketing.

While many of us think of a spiderweb having many radius lines coming out from the centre, some webs have far less than others.

Some of the lines are shorter, and others are key to helping build strength in the full web. The lines closest to the anchor are key (this would be your website and your core social media platform) while others just help create a full picture and allow you to increase your chances to catch your people.

As you begin to build your own web, you may find you have less radius lines than others. Focus on doubling back on these lines, making them strong, then gradually add in other lines as you become more confident and used to your web.

The Capture Spiral

Starting at the outside, and moving your way in, you move around and around, and create the capture spiral. For us as business owners, this means sharing your content. This gets your business noticed, helps people connect with you, feel nurtured and then at the centre, become yours. As you move closer to the centre, we want to make sure the web gets stickier and sticker, and harder to escape. The content becomes more in depth, adding deeper value. It might include offers to spend more time with you, and interact with you. Eventually they'll be invited to buy from you and will be ready.

There is more room on the outside of the web to share "get noticed" content, and less room as you move in. We need to remember to share more of this type of content than content that promotes our services. The stickiest content (the "BUY MY STUFF" stuff) is shared with the least people of all.

There are no dangerous gaps on our web, and the capture spiral keeps our visitors safe. It helps them trust us, and move closer. Our consistency in message and scheduling of content is the silk the capture spiral is made of.

The Frame Thread

As we build our web, we may discover overlaps between different platforms, such as a link between our Instagram account and our webinars. We can create bridge lines (links) to help these connect together, to make it easy for people to take quick shortcuts without having to leave the web we've made.

The U-Turn

Sometimes we want someone to stay on our radius line, so instead of moving the spiral closer, we'll U-turn and create a few extra lines between two radii, to make that bond stronger, and help our visitors stay around on that radius line a bit longer (maybe it's TikTok, maybe it's your website. We're sneaky spiders like that.)

The Hub

This is where you save your stickiest silk. This is your most compelling content, that's going to help them decide to pay you for hanging out on your web. Our Hub is our stories, private messages, or emails, our Zoom calls, our sales sequence. It's where we put most of our one-to-one energy, and each person is ready for it, because they've moved onto your web, down your radius lines, around your capture spiral and now they're ready for you.

I WANT YOU TO BUILD A WEB

I want you to imagine there's a beautiful web above you. (The spider who made it was kind, let me borrow it and is currently on a holiday, so relax, they are nowhere near their web!)

I want you to see the radius lines coming from the centre, and the capture spiral of the spider silk moving around and around them, from the outside to right to the centre.

Now reach up and take the centre of that web and pull it down. (Spider silk is elastic and very strong—it won't break) As you pull it down, you'll see it makes a funnel shape. But with a difference.

Think of every radius of the web as an entry point, or platform. Now let's use that shape and think about people using it as a path to get to you, right in the Hub of that web.

This funnel has lots of different entry points. Your job is to make sure you've got enough to attract people in different spaces.

The spiral of the web is your future customers' walkway, with each level allowing a place to rest if needed. We're not in a rush to push people along. We're a patient spider. We know they will come to the Hub when they are ready.

It's possible to move across the threads, experiencing different platforms.

Sometimes someone will enter at the top, and scurry along one of the spokes straight to the centre. They're acting exactly the way they would if it was a funnel with a slippery slide down. But most of the time, they move up and down, around and around that web. They find pockets where other people are hanging there, and spend time there. They move closer, then further away again.

They don't walk in straight lines, but it's ok, because they're in your web.

They'll make it to you when they're ready.

You just need to keep on giving them reasons to come closer.

YOUR CONTENT WEB IS JUST THE SAME

One of the most exciting parts of creating a content web is you allow people to find you where they hang out. Your future clients and customers will come to your web at different points, depending on where you've spun your web.

Most of them will enter from one of the outer edges where there is less commitment, less personal interaction and they can watch for a while, and check you're one of those kind spiders they're looking for.

Sometimes you'll get someone who jumps right in and skips the outer parts. If they've come with a person who's worked with you before, or knows you, they'll feel safe enough to jump into the middle tiers of the web right away. They may also do this if they're a risk taker, or they're jumping from someone's web.

It's rare for most people to jump right into the centre (the Hub), and be ready to buy, and if they do, you'll often have to spend time in sales meetings building rapport and trust. This is something you won't need to do with people who've hung out on your web for a while. You've already let them take their time developing their trust, and they're ready.

As we explained before, each radius of your web is a type of marketing. One will be your website, the rest social media platforms, marketing activities and email marketing that helps draw people in.

Some have heavier lines on the outer of the spiral, perfect for attracting the new people onto your web and less as the person gets closer. (For instance, Pinterest is a powerful source for initial interest, but it is harder to help build engagement and community the closer people come to the centre and make a purchase.)

Others will be sparse at the top and have a whole lot going on closer to the Hub. If webinars are part of your content marketing web, they will only be an initial entry point to risk takers, people in intense pain (and you're meeting them "just at the right time") or people who've been told to attend by someone else already on your web.

No matter when someone enters our web, they get to choose the pace of the journey to your Hub. If someone enters the web halfway to the Hub, they'll still move around the web in exactly the same way as if they had entered on the outer parts of a web. Building trust takes the time it takes, and each person has slightly different ways to check the trust lines you've built. It's not our job to choose their direction, or their pace. We're just here making all the paths we can to make it easier to find us at the Hub.

Our job is to be patient. Trust in the stickiness of the web. And resist pouncing on our new visitors to bite. In other words, we need to be that kind spider. Sometimes that means showing people what we're really like.

CHAPTER 3
YOU ARE A UNIQUE SPIDER

HOW I FOUND MY PEOPLE

IF THERE'S A PEOPLE PLEASER ANONYMOUS, I'D BE A FOUNDING MEMBER. IT used to be a constant struggle to be myself. I didn't want my real self to cost someone else a lesser experience of what they wanted me to be. Later on, we're going to talk about burnt toast (burnt chop) syndrome and how desperately I used to work to fit in.

Somewhere along the way, my idea of who I was became so blurred and undefined that I didn't know myself anymore. I'd find myself getting into stuff that wasn't in line with my values, or hanging out with people who were into things I wasn't. It felt easier to go along with what they wanted to do, rather than cause a ruckus.

I thought that doing this would make me more likeable.

In some ways, initially it did. People liked whatever chameleon image of me they got, my reflection of them as I saw it.

The problem was that it was a veneer of me. The more they'd interact with me, the faster they'd notice the veneer slip a little bit. Instead of authentic Rachel, they had pretend Rachel. It's what I thought they wanted, because it fitted in with them, but in the end it just felt fake to everyone.

There is one thing far worse than finding out that someone is not one of your people. And that is thinking someone was your people, then discovering they were only pretending, and feeling you've been duped.

I didn't think that was what I was doing. I didn't wake up one day and think "I'm going to pretend to be like that person so they'll like me" It was more like "I can be what they need from me, even if it's not really me, because this way they'll be happier."

I'd do it again and again. Each time I'd start off as myself, then adapt and alter myself to be what I thought they wanted until I was no longer me. I was doing it on all fronts, in all places and it was exhausting. It was also highly ineffective in terms of finding my people.

I'd like to say the first time I crashed and burned I figured out where I went wrong, but I didn't.

I just invested more time into trying to be what I thought people wanted.

Here's the problem with this. Beyond the fact it was having a terrible impact on my self-confidence, and life in general, it also made it very difficult to find my people.

How can you find your people when they can't see you under all that veneer?

When we had a massive crash and burn with our business, that led to Identify changing our whole outlook, I realised that a big part of the problem had been me.

How could the best people for me, for us as a business, find us, and know us for what we do best, if we don't know it, and share it consistently first?

It would have been great to learn this thirty years ago but I didn't. I hit rock bottom, broken, hurt and feeling very attacked for all the hard work I'd been putting in. While sitting there, I sat and I tried to write a list of who the real me was, but I didn't get very far. I truly wasn't sure of what I was, or what I liked, or who I connected best with. I just knew I had to find it.

I'VE GOT MY EYES ON YOU

Unlike spiders, some of whom have eight eyes, others six, and some none at all, I have one pair of eyes and I've learnt it counts where I let them set their attention.

In finding the real me, I realised I'd been trying to be "someone". Pretty much anybody but the person I was if truth be told! In my quest to be someone, I went everywhere. I got invited to a lot of events and parties filled with beautiful people, alcohol, and canapes. (On the other side of this life was an inability to pay my rent, but that's another story!)

When you want to be somebody, you want everybody to love you. And it's all about finding the important people in the room to connect with who will help you be loved a little more by a lot more people.

At these events, I'd keep the room scan on automatic. No matter who I was talking to, I was alert, and scanning the room for the next person to talk to, who might be a good person to connect with and interact with.

It meant that I was never 100% present with the person who I was talking with. Not that they often noticed as they were also distracted and scanning past my shoulder. You could go a whole night, talk to a huge amount of people, and still not really have connected with anyone. I was the most socially active I'd ever been. I was filled with anxiety and felt incredibly alone.

I took my sister along to one of these events, and she caught me doing the room scan while talking to her. And, as all good sisters do, she firmly told me off. After getting defensive I realised she had a point. It had become such second nature, I hadn't noticed I was doing it.

She had looked me in the eye, talked to me alone, and reminded me that that is how a relationship works.

I began to notice everyone else at these parties were also scanning the room while I was talking. They would look at me but a little to my left, or my right so they could check who was behind me. Or they'd talk to me, then pick up their phone and start replying to a funny tweet or text.

This had contributed to my empty feelings. I had the sensation of being social, and interacting, and yet there was no real desire to create long-term connections.

I've seen the same behaviour at networking events. You get asked a question as a warm-up and while you are answering, you know they're just waiting for you to stop so they can reel into their elevator pitch. They're not really listening. They're pretending.

You can't be loved by everyone. And sometimes when we're seeking that, we don't notice we're not really loved by anyone.

When I began to let go of the need to work the room and respect the one person in front of me, life changed. It got quieter. And the circle got (a lot) smaller. And the parties got fewer.

But the relationships grew richer. I became more than just a somebody to some people. And as someone totally out of the loop these days, I love not trying to be anyone else than me.

Social media is a big noisy party. The world is a fast hot mess of distraction and noise. It's tempting to stand out by trying to be everything you think the world needs. When we do that, we're going to look busy and popular but no one's going to want to come sit with us, in the quiet, and choose us.

When we write our posts, when we create our content, and we talk to our audience, it will always have more impact if it's written to the one person standing in front of you. Forget the crowds. It's just you and one person. Having a conversation.

When we relinquish the desire to be noticed by everyone, to see how far our reach will go, how many people will notice us, that is when the magic begins to happen. That one person will know you've got your eyes on them. They'll know you've listened to what they've said. They'll know that you want to have a relationship with them. And they'll love you for it.

When they respond (because they will respond), you'll be there to let them know you listened back.

We can't build our tribe of many, until we've learned to honour the connection with that one person. Before you create any content, remember that ideal person you are talking to and say quietly "I've got my eyes on you".

When I realised I craved a connection with people who liked me, the flawed, quirky, imperfect me, everything changed. Including finding it so easy to walk away from the people who didn't like me. I released them to find the right people for them.

YOUR FACE STRENGTHENS THE TRUST BRIDGE

If I had a dollar for every client who told me they didn't want to show their face on social media, I'd be able to retire! Using photos of ourselves in our marketing as small business owners is one of the single biggest obstacles many of my clients have (especially the women).

As we all become more disconnected from everyday interactions in a store, an office, or public, re-fabricating that connection with a photo becomes a very important marketing tool. A photo of you on your brand page will nearly always get double or more engagement than a photo of something you sell.

I know you may not be a fan of coming out and showing your face. You might even not let your significant others take a photo of you, let alone post them on social media! The idea of putting yourself out there is a terrifying notion.

One of my biggest blocks was that it felt narcissistic. I felt I might turn into a massive egomaniac. I also would happily film myself but then pick my appearance to pieces while watching the reply. I have perpetually unkempt hair! It was a jarring reminder that that is not the image we carry of ourselves in our own head.

My defining moment was booking a brand shoot. My photographer Nykie was relaxed and encouraging. She liked it when I goofed off! I was so excited to see the images. But when they arrived I was distraught. All I could see was my flaws. I posted the worst images in a group and someone said, "I'd book you just because of that expression".

I threw back my shoulders, took a deep breath and decided to go all in and use my photos everywhere. Engagement on my posts surged. The only comments I got on my posts were about my smile and energy.

People started to message me and ask how to be as confident as me. Some got inspired to put photos of themselves more in their social media posts. Those who were laughing near me seemed to be laughing with me. (That's what I'm telling myself anyway!)

That first brand shoot was a defining line in the sand where I showed up, and it turned a light on in our business. I work with my husband, and a team, but I'm the face of our business. I now use my face everywhere; in my event ads, my speaking slides, and even my printed materials. It took a few years before I stopped feeling I had to apologise for having my face as part of my brand. Now, I make videos dressed up as a road cone. How things have changed.

If I wear the same clothes in meetings, or at events that are in my brand shoot, some people remark it makes them feel they can trust me more. They feel they already know me. In my events, people have said it felt they already had rapport with me before I started.

People would mention as they became clients that seeing photos of me helped them choose me to work with. In a sea of thousands of other marketers, I somehow reflected back what they needed. It's helped us attract the right people for us.

Of course, equally, I was repelling people all the time too. For the first time in my life I didn't care about that. I was finding my people. Now

I'm so busy with them, I've got no time or energy to worry about the people who really don't like me.

Our business has grown into one where every client we have is the perfect fit for us and what we're good at. My photos have helped act as a filter to draw in the ones that respond best to what we do best.

Flipping the story, when I outed my creative zany fun side, in all my ageing plus-size glory, I gained an amazing community of people who weirdly love it, and are motivated by it.

But even better, it's motivated me to show up and be myself, to explore the things I really love to do, to spend my time and energy with people who get and like me, and not be so affected by all the others who don't.

Not everyone will like us (or me). I truly understand why we fear this. I did for a very very long time. But when we show ourselves as we are, the right people like us. And that's all that counts. For business. And for life.

YOU'VE NEVER KILLED A MAN WITH YOUR FACE

(That I know of.)

If you're reading this and saying to me "Rachel, you don't understand. People will just not like my face", then I've got some very bad news for you and your face.

You've got a choice. Get over this idea that you have to have the right kind of face, or lose out on sales. The more you show your face, the better it will be for your business. Even if it's not a pretty face.

If you can also bring yourself to open your mouth, and record the words coming out of your face, you will find that is also better for your business. It doesn't even really matter what you sell. Your face talking to a camera works.

Long before I did the shoot with Nykie, I had to do some promotional work for a short-term gig on morning television as a relationship advisor after a book I wrote on dating came out. They spent hours making me look perfect in thick makeup, studio lights, borrowed clothes and then edited the images on top of that. I looked amazing. And nothing like me.

Then every week, I'd turn up to the studio in my beautiful (again gifted) designer clothes, and they'd spend about thirty minutes doing my hair and putting a whole heap of makeup on my face, and then I'd go talk for about two and a half minutes and then it was done. Go make a cup of tea during the break and be late back, and you'd miss it.

With the clothes, the hair, the makeup, the lights, the soundbites and the cameras I looked as good as I was ever going to get. I felt good.

But even then, I ripped myself to pieces when I watched myself on replay. I learned one of the biggest secrets of video creation: Don't watch the video of yourself until you've had a lot of people tell you you were awesome first. You're going to need those comments when your brain starts tearing your appearance apart.

A few years back I caught up with my friend Johnny (who happens to be one of my favourite people of all time). We were in his office and we got talking about video. He opened up his video travel bag and unloaded this set of awesome kit he carries with him everywhere to take videos of himself.

It was hilarious because, at that point, he wasn't doing video. He was just ready IN CASE HE DID. His block, like mine and nearly everyone else's was: What if I look like a complete idiot on camera? Recently, Johnny's been using video.

He's awesome at it. He's the same heartfelt magic person I know and love on camera as he is in person. When I asked him what his breakthrough moment was, he said his partner had told him: Just record it and upload it. Do this for three days straight. DO NOT WATCH IT FIRST.

The theory was similar to what I learned back in the days of my all too brief "huge" TV career—It's easier to watch yourself back after other people have said you were awesome.

Even then, it's still not fun. Your inner critic will go into overdrive. Remember that what you are seeing is what others see. Your voice is the voice they hear. They don't see the person you are in the mirror or hear how you sound in your head.

They are used to you. No one is recoiling from you in abject horror as you walk into a room. No one is running from you, hands over their ears crying "STOP! Your voice, it's all wrong!" No one is dying from your face.

The more you relax into the fact that you are not causing mass death when you create video, or pop a photo of yourself in a post or an email, the easier it becomes to just be yourself.

Now, I look down the lens of the camera, and I pretend it's YOU looking at me. And I talk to you.

If I'm too old, too round, too noisy, too weird or too ugly for you, if who I am is not what you want to work with, if my voice is going to cause you to block your ears with fancy cheese, if I'm going to kill a man with my face—well I'd rather we sorted that BEFORE we meet in person.

(And to my knowledge, I've never killed a man with my face. With confidence I'll say you have not either.)

HEFFALUMP: IT'S OK TO BE ONE

While we're talking learning curves, let's acknowledge that all change is painful and learning can often hurt. I'm currently on a huge learning curve as I work on my own skills around video and content. I push, I get frustrated and I get tired. I have also been known to throw a temper tantrum or two. (We talk about how we're all adult toddlers later on.)

It would be very unfair for me to expect you to read this book, put it down, and then magically start to create incredible content. I mean I'm good, but I'm not THAT good!

For me, writing content is as natural as breathing. I can think of entire paragraphs in my head, get out my laptop, and put on some music and the sentences dance together, words crossing over each other, ducking in and out to craft the sentences I want to weave together to tell you a story.

I can write a thousand words in twenty minutes if I'm passionate enough. Because it's now so much a part of me, it's easy to forget just how disappointed my teachers were in me at school for being unable to write as much as I spoke.

I'd describe myself as a nimble writing gazelle.

You? You might be a heffalump[1].

I'm a heffalump when it comes to running.

I discovered running when I turned forty after I decided I would like to run a half-marathon for my birthday. I undiscovered it again after I hurt my back and now I am a walker, but for a brief short time I learned why running is so addictive. There is this rush, from "I'm going to die, this is the most horrendous thing I've ever done in my entire life, why was I so stupid?", to "I found my stride", to "I think I could just run forever" (forever for me was about an hour!)

I felt like a gazelle when I was running. In truth, I looked like a heffalump.

I'm not a natural runner. I'm always up for a sprained ankle on uneven ground, I run in an ungainly way, and I spend half the run trying to remember what normal gait is. Perhaps if I ran for years, this would change. Perhaps I'd transform into a gazelle. Or maybe I'd just be a very fit heffalump.

Here's the thing. My runs did not look pretty, but they were still a run. The more often I went for one, the faster and more confident I got.

You may never find content creation comfortable. You may decide to outsource it once you understand it and where your role sits in content creation. If you do, make sure you find the best gazelle you can afford.

But whether you do, or just stick making it with your heffalump fingers and heffalump brain, you'll still see results.

I promise it's ok to be a heffalump. Heffalumps still get things done.

LOOKING STUPID IS EASIER WHEN THE AUDIENCE IS SMALL

Yesterday I tried to stream to multiple platforms at once with a new app. I like to make things challenging. So I advertised it and got a bit of a buzz. On the day of the livestream, I freaked out at the pressure I'd put myself under, but I went live regardless. I did wonder why I saw no questions, until I discovered I'd set the live to "private" so I was doing it completely alone. In hindsight the mistake was a huge gift. An audience of none is great for a first go!

When you begin to show up as the spider who's created this beautiful web, it can be terrifying. Just remember it's unlikely many people will see your first attempts. You might do a video and only three people watch it. You've got the time to become more confident while the audience builds over time.

Of course, I can't promise a lack of audience.

Last year I got an email from a client with the subject line "You Lied!"

Panic? Why yes, I did. And then I read the email…

You said when I did my first story that no one would see it, that for the first few weeks it's just good practice and it doesn't matter how bad it is…

Well, I did my first 'showing my actual face' story this afternoon.

YOU LIED!

Every man and his bloody dog has seen it and messaged me and commented on it, including people I haven't heard from for years!

(I might add, it took me most of the afternoon to do, so it's probably quite gratifying in a way that it did not go unnoticed.)

After my heart rate slowed down, I was so happy for her. After this she persevered and kept going. As the owner of four retail stores, it's allowed her to show up to her customers across all the stores, along with building her online store sales.

I was watching her this morning, and she's now so relaxed in front of the camera. She's smiling, her dry humour is coming through and we're seeing her personality shine. She knows she can attribute sales to her videos, and as she develops more confidence, that will continue.

Even a year later, I'm still SO proud that she took that first step. And I think she's forgiven me now. (Paula, if you're reading this, I hope you have!)

With the image of a completed spider web in your mind, and a reminder to be a kind spider, let's start to build your web. It all starts with finding the right anchor point.

PART TWO
THE ANCHOR POINT

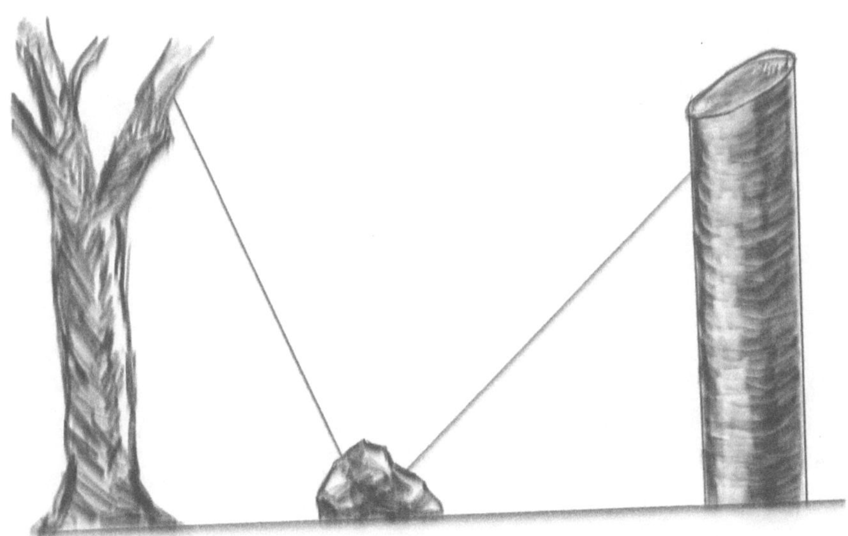

CHAPTER 4
WE START WITH AN ANCHOR

IF I WAS STARTING OUR BUSINESS AGAIN, AND WANTED TO BUILD IT RIGHT from day one, I'd have followed all the steps to find my ideal anchor right from the start.

But I'm a woman of action, impulsive, impatient, and learn from my mistakes far more readily than my planning. I know I'm not the only one.

Small businesses are often built like a multigenerational family holiday home. (In New Zealand we call them a bach, or a crib.) You start with a one room building with an outhouse and an outside shower and then over the years extra rooms and amenities are added, depending on years of plenty, family growth and the different tastes of every decade.

It's a beautiful testament to the story of growth and change. It's also chaotic, lacks flow and is vastly different to what would have resulted if you'd carefully mapped out a plan for long-term growth right from the beginning.

As someone who built a business like a poorly thought out bach, I know sometimes it's better to remove your most precious possessions, burn it all to the ground and plan again from scratch. I will share later why we had to do this, and what the outcome was. If you're living in that complicated bach of a business, you may need to remodel a few rooms, destroy a whole wing or even do as we did, and start almost from scratch again.

Wherever you sit, walk through the following steps to check how your business is set up for growth, before we learn how to amplify your message.

When a spider is planning a web, they first go hunting for just the right spot. They make sure it's starting from stable ground like a rock, a large branch or the side of our home. If they get this first step wrong, the whole web's structure will be weaker.

We need to build a sticky, strong web that withstands the unexpected. When the anchor point is a good one, we won't have to keep scurrying around trying to fix other parts of our business. The anchor point helps us stay grounded in what's important to us, and builds a healthy business.

A good place to start is in determining your core values.

CHAPTER 5

OUR THREE CORE VALUES

WE HAVE THREE CORE VALUES AT IDENTIFY THAT HELP US WITH EVERY aspect of our business. Soon I'm going to share our redemption story (or how we demolished the bach and rebuilt). It all started by us exploring what values we wanted to live, breathe, and become known for.

When I started Identify I didn't put too much time into thinking about our core values. This was partly because Identify was going to be, like all my other businesses, a solopreneur freelancing business. So my values were in me. I didn't feel I needed to spend time defining them.

I knew what my values were. As we grew, and the business changed, I made two really bad assumptions. I thought people would automatically know what my values were, and I assumed their values would be the same as mine. I was catastrophically wrong on both counts.

Because I hadn't taken the time to define my values and then build our business around it, Identify just absorbed every team member's values into it as well. I made assumption after assumption about expected behaviour, how we related to clients, how we would work based around my values. I didn't talk about our business values, I just expected they'd know. By not making these values clear to others joining our team, I set them up for failure when they didn't meet them.

Before starting Identify I worked for another business who had used their company values like a weapon. One of their core values was FAMILY. And yes, they did live this value, but it was one of those dysfunctional families where the rules change all the time, you get the wooden spoon if you are naughty and there is definitely one favourite child! Even as their favourite child a lot of the time, my idea of family was very different from that.

I didn't want to just pick three words from the air and say, "here are our values." Core values are the values people associate with you, even if they're not directly expressed. They will impact the way you market your business, sell, onboard new clients, look after them through that process, and then keep in touch with them well after the job is done.

We recently got some case studies written about our work with clients. The writer came back to me at the end of all her interviews and said "I can tell you exactly what your values are" because each client shared the same three themes with her as they talked about us. This is a sign that our values are lived.

Values cannot be inspirational. They are not what you are aiming for. They are who you are. Whatever you stand by needs to be something you can deliver on consistently. While they can be a single word of a simple phrase, it's super important you define what they look like. How would a customer know that was your value? How would you describe it to a potential new team member? What difference do they make when you inevitably make a mistake and need to put it right? How will they shape the way you set up your working day, your week, your year?

Because I co-own my business with my husband Rod, we worked together to create three shared values. Our values shape everything, including why I'm writing this book.

OUR FIRST VALUE: KEEP IT SIMPLE

If I had a favourite value this would be it.

Simple is not the same as easy. A good content marketing plan is nearly always simple. It doesn't mean doing all the work to execute the plan is easy. Simple means that you understand it, and you can see how it all fits together.

Simple means we talk in everyday language with our clients. We don't try to confuse people with a bunch of jargon. If we do need to use industry words and definitions, for instance when talking about Search Engine Optimisation (SEO), we try to find ways to explain it with stories and examples.

I don't want anyone to feel stupid simply because I want them to think I'm intelligent. I don't need to be the smartest person in the room. As a marketing strategist, I work with business owners who may not understand marketing, but are experts in what they do. I don't need to show my knowledge is more important than theirs. If there's a simple way to explain something I'll use it. All I want is to see the light go on when they understand an idea or a technique for the first time.

Having "keep it simple" as a value makes us check in with our clients and check we are helping them learn the best way.

Last year I worked with a dyslexic client who found our lists and written explanations too much to process. I realised our strategies were pretty wordy. I turned most of the instructional content into infographics and flowcharts he could follow and use to implement his marketing. Our clients now all get these, alongside the written content. I find I often use them too to check my work. We also added video walkthroughs for people who like to learn through observation.

Keeping it simple is not just about client care. When we're setting goals, we check in. Is this the simplest path forward? What can we do to make it simpler? We use it to check our processes. We use it when determining our core offers. We assess the apps and online solutions we use and ask ourselves "is this keeping it simple?"

While I lived and breathed "keep it simple" when teaching, seeing how we could use it throughout our business has been liberating. I'm not always able to work out how to simplify a big idea by myself. I know the end goal but I also like the distractible pathway to get there, with the twists, turns and exciting developments.

I've learned to love how Rod, and others in our team, can take my end goal and find a simpler way to get it done. (I did find it annoying at first as I liked my complicated and unplanned processes!) When we keep it simple, the business operates better and our clients get a better result.

OUR SECOND VALUE: 'FOLLOW THE CUSTOMER'

We made several almost prescient changes to our business just before the pandemic changed the way business worked.

We'd already been using Zoom for our sales meetings. As we grew, we realised we were wasting a lot of downtime driving (or flying) to meetings. We'd started to encourage people to work with us via Zoom or at our offices to maximise everyone's time. This resulted in us delivering better results to our clients, without making someone pay for all the extra travel time.

We also made a paid course of ours completely free. The Marketing Toolbox was an online strategy programme that we ran as a membership programme. In January 2020 I felt an urgency to make this platform completely free, and to give it away as a gift that had no upsell to it. This felt completely counter intuitive. It was partly to help address the growing needs of potential customers who came to work with us and found they could not afford to. I didn't like sending these people away with nothing. I knew if I grew their business, they may be ready to work with us one day. If nothing else, they'd have a great experience with us virtually.

At that time, we also struggled to keep our school updated with all the digital marketing changes along with our current client work. I wasn't able to keep up to date with creating constant content, so making it free alleviated some of the pressure and expectations of continuous creation.

Little did we know the world was about to change and this free tool would then be used by hundreds of stressed business owners, suddenly with plenty of time to work on their business, but little money to pay for it.

Last year I knew it was time to change this again. To be honest, I was told to change it by my clients and community. They felt our free value to paid offer balance was out. They demanded changes! So, we rebuilt the course, updated it with all our new infographics and renamed it My MAP IT Marketing Strategy School. We officially retired The Marketing Toolbox. Our "follow the customer" value listened to our customers and delivered. I did ensure all our past enrolled students got access to it free—because that also fitted our values.

In 2020, we identified that the action plans we wrote for our clients often left them with more questions and sticking points than we felt comfortable with. While every strategy is different, many of the core actions are the same from plan to plan. We wanted to simplify the learning for clients who struggled with the "how to" of marketing.

For me, setting up an Instagram account is simple. For many of our clients it is anything but easy! So we developed a portal our clients get free lifetime access to that helps take them through all of the steps they need to take to make their own page, step up accounts, write content and more.

We don't have to do this. We know we could just tell them to Google it or check out YouTube. We also know our clients already trust us, are busy, need help, and they may not know which advice is best to follow. We made it our job to meet their needs.

Following the customer has led to us discovering new opportunities. From online webinars to physical marketing resources, to podcasts and more. All of which has led us to growth in our business. Following the customer has meant finding more of them too.

OUR THIRD VALUE: ADD VALUE

I lied. THIS is my favourite value. (It's so hard to choose when you love them all!)

Last year, Rod and I had one of our regular "where are we headed and are we moving to make that happen" meetings. I highly recommend blocking out time to have these meetings with a business partner, coach or even yourself.

We made a huge amount of progress and then Rod asked me a question. "What work lights Rachel up and how do we make her work week reflect that?"

The answer was instant. If I'm in a place where I'm adding value, I'm happy.

For me, adding value is creating content like this book. It's speaking. It's helping people get excited about what marketing can do for their business. It's making videos. It's writing blogs, posts, planning imagery that helps people learn and get excited about what is possible, helping them learn it the best way for them.

If we're going to do anything, it needs to add value. If we can't work out how to make that happen for our ideal customer, we don't do it. Even if everyone else does.

When you bought this book or audio book, you also get access to the free guide that comes with it. That's us adding value.

Our podcast, our Facebook group, our free (and paid) events and webinars, our YouTube videos and blogs, our posts on social media platforms everywhere—all of these things are designed to add value.

We believe adding value to people who are getting to know us or haven't worked with us yet is really important. Our posts aren't a secret trapdoor spider lair designed to entangle you in a pit of despair once you step into it. They are a hint of what you'll get if you work with us, but they are a free gift even if you never work with us. EVER.

That's how adding value works.

We equally believe in adding value to people we are already working with. And I think businesses often get that confused. We spend time making sure our current/past clients also have added value, so they get extras and client-only portals that only they can access. And because of that, we build a lifetime relationship with them. We're not interested in short term relationships. We're in it for the long haul.

We don't have to do that. We don't offer a lot of ongoing work, or retainer arrangements. Our business is built around one-off bits of work. We could very easily just decide to NOT. But that would not fit in with our values.

When you define your values, they become the anchor point the rest of your content web is built on. This is your first step.

CHAPTER 6
HOW TO DEFINE YOUR OWN VALUES

HERE'S MY TOP ADVICE ON HOW TO USE SOCIAL MEDIA TO GROW YOUR business.

In every post, before you hit PUBLISH, ask yourself "does this add value to the reader?" AND/OR "does this show MY values?"

If 90% of your posts do this, you'll be ahead of everyone else in your industry because people will connect with you, trust you and want to work with you.

Whether you work them out, declare them or not, your values already impact your business in some way.

Soon I'll share how this impacted Identify. When I look back to the dark days of my business, I know my values were not aligned with my team. This led us to treat our clients in a haphazard way, meant we had mixed communication around how we talked to each other and our clients, and created dissonance in everything we did. It created an unhealthy business in every sense of the word.

This was not my team's fault. This was mine. I did not set my values clearly, right from the start.

I don't believe there is one value that is better than another. A competitor can live by a completely different set of values and still deliver excellent results for their clients. It is difficult to deliver great results to a client when your values aren't aligned with theirs. So you can't just pinch someone else's values to set as your anchor point.

As you get better at showing your values in your marketing, the quality of your clients will improve. People who align themselves with our values will be drawn to us.

I often suggest limiting yourself to three core values. It might be because I have an easily distractible brain but I find more than three often means you forget one. Nothing says "that's not really a value" if you've got to check your website or a sign on the wall to remember it. A real value is one that is tattooed on your heart, your "go-to" for each decision you make.

As a small business owner, your values will likely align with your personal values. Even if you have a team, your values should align with how you best live your life or you'll exhaust yourself trying to keep up with a value system that you don't really believe in. Owning a business is hard enough without adding that pressure on.

Years before I was a marketing strategist I worked in leadership and team development. Let's forget for a moment the irony that I'd never built my own team before this, and when I finally did, the first attempt was disastrous. I guess I prove the adage "those who can't, teach"? Anyway, I was pretty good at helping teams work together to work out their team values.

If you want to include your team in this process, define your own first. No matter how incredible your team is, the business is yours. The values start with you. Once you've defined them, work out how to show these to your team, and help everyone understand what these values mean in the everyday life of your business.

If you don't define the values of your business, someone else in your team, or a strong willed client, will. This creates immense risk, and may grow your business in the wrong direction.

HERE'S SEVERAL STEPS YOU CAN TAKE TO DEFINE YOUR OWN VALUES

There are piles of books written by values experts that can take this far deeper than me. However, here's a few simple steps we used to determine ours

Most values coaches start with asking you to sift through a long list of words to find the ones that pop out. I used to carry bags of four hundred words into my seminars to do the same process and I would still do this with someone who had no idea about what values were most important for them.

When it came to us working out our values as a business we skipped this step because we'd both sat through enough of these sessions to have an awareness of our own personal values. It is a very good way to filter your ideas if you have never considered your values. So do this first.

As we were already aware of our personal values, we jumped straight into how we'd convey these to our ideal clients.

How to check your offer fits your values:

- **Look at what you do best. What is it that you can consistently deliver to people over and over again?**

For us, it was straight forward marketing strategies, clear action plans, explaining things without jargon and helping people learn how to do marketing themselves.

- **What do you find difficult to deliver consistently, or have little interest in focussing on?**

For me it was making everything super pretty with fancy graphs. This means we don't create epically colourful pretty plans, which saves us extra design time and keeps our costs down, which we can pass on to our customers.

We also didn't enjoy spending hours in commuter traffic. I also didn't enjoy losing touch with our clients as the team grew.

- **If it was only ever you in the business, what would you want people to say about you and your work?**

We didn't want to build a business on skills that Rod or I couldn't do ourselves if needed, incase we needed to jump in and help at some point as the business grew

We also knew that it was up to us to determine what good looked like. Identifying this also helped us work out how we would show we were delivering that to our customers. We couldn't add value if we only understood the basics.

- **Look at the businesses you love and why. What makes the experience with them so enjoyable? Is it something you also know you can deliver?**

For us it was people who delivered when they said they would, who followed a brief, showed up on time, were easy to talk to, didn't make us feel like stupid and added a little extra that surpised and delighted us.

- **Look at the customers you've done your best work with.**

We noticed that our best work was done with people who liked direct, straight up feedback, who were ready to put time aside for their marketing, liked paying us, and wanted to understand how it all worked

- **Take a look at the clients who didn't work out.**

As we did this exercise when our business was broken, we had more of these that we wanted. Instead of looking at them all, We looked at the people we knew we had delivered our best work to and it was still not well received. We found these people often had a long list of people who had also not made the grade, found it hard to trust us, wanted a plan but wasn't ready to change habits to make the changes.

Action: It's your turn.

If you know you need to define your values, to help find a better anchor point, block out time to work through your values. Your web will not be strong unless you work this out.

CHAPTER 7
FACING MARKETING OVERWHELM AND AVOIDANCE

EVER BITTEN OFF MORE THAN YOU CAN CHEW?

*Yeah... me neither**

**LIES!!!!*

I like to try to get it all done. Say yes to things. Pop cool extra things in my diary.

I'm learning to:

- *Make room for NOTHING*
- *Take time to breathe*
- *Remember that I don't need to cram it all in*

A great anchor point is not enough when building your web. I work with a lot of businesses who I call "best kept secrets". They have grown on the power of their anchor point, creating a tiny web of a website, a little used Facebook page, and the odd radio ad here and there.

They have incredible businesses. They have a large proportion of repeat business, and word of mouth business. Their customers stick around on their sticky web and never want to leave.

All of this is excellent. Until it comes time to grow more, protect themselves from a new competitor, or change their offer. They need to build a bigger web. To do that, they need to find a bigger space to build, which might mean they need to prioritise time, move some budget into marketing, and face the moment of marketing overwhelm.

I don't think I've met a business owner yet who hasn't felt overwhelmed when it comes to marketing at some point. Including myself.

I used to find the whole job, on top of my "real" job of working with our clients, and helping our team, just too much. Like many business owners, for a long time I worked on our marketing in the "extra" time of evenings, weekends and lunch breaks, instead of counting it as essential work.

As a true sucker for punishment, I seek out marketing overwhelm every year. I want to remind myself of the feelings you get when trying to learn a new platform, technique or embedded a habit. It reminds me why it's so easy to give up, and what it feels like to learn marketing skills while trying to run your business.

That self-punishment aside, I sometimes get overwhelmed when we're launching a new offer, or during our very busy months. I've not perfected the art of never feeling overwhelmed, but I've found there are several steps I take for myself and my clients that work well.

WORK OUT IF IT'S MARKETING THAT'S THE PROBLEM

As a small business owner, you are juggling a pile of balls that move all over the place as soon as they leave your hands. We've worked with business owners who are running a business while also dealing with huge personal or family concerns. There's been issues with staffing, managing rapid growth, or just trying to ensure you've got enough to cover your rent for the month. Sometimes, the owner is on the precipice of burnout and everything is suffering.

While I'm always going to be a cheerleader for marketing, sometimes there are more important factors at play. You can't build a web surrounded by uncontrollable fires. If that's you, my recommendation is to step back. As you do, recognise it's a conscious decision to step back from all the marketing you could be doing. Give yourself a timeline to come back to it.

Part of my overwhelm comes from me sacrificing my own time to think, unwind and take a step away from the business to learn. This only leads to me becoming highly unpleasant to be around or having a minor meltdown because someone forgot to unload the dishwasher at home.

It's not sustainable to use weekends and nights to work on your marketing. Your business should be able to sustain you having some of your working week to focus just on your marketing. (We'll cover this more in Part Three.)

ACCEPT IT'S FOR THE LONG GAME

Consistent marketing over a long period of time makes your sales process simpler. Once your marketing starts to work, the results from it feel effortless. But that feeling comes from a lot of time, patience, and sticking to your plan!

When we're focussed on putting out fires, we forget to focus on our long-term strategy. Both need our time now, and the benefits of sticking to your plan can feel like a leap of faith, as you've got to put in the work before you see the results. You will need to trust the process.

(As an aside, try writing a book. It's spending hours collecting thoughts, ideas and organising them and hoping someone is going to read or listen to it someday! It's definitely a long-term plan…!)

We normally say that it's at least six weeks before you'll see any results from any new marketing activity. This can feel like an age when you are taking time away from your current quick fixes such as jumping on a pile of cold calls, or turning up at a market to invest in a promised future.

If you need to keep everything going, and plan for the future, there will be an initial squeeze on your time and energy. It might feel uncomfortable and hard, but it will pay off.

BOOK THE TIME IN YOUR DIARY

If it's not in your diary, it's going to be happening after hours (if it happens at all.)

In terms of time, I normally say allocating four hours per week for your marketing is about right for a solopreneur, plus another day a month to analyse what's going on, and plan for the following month. When you start creating content, you might need a little more time to get your foundations right. However, people are often surprised at how much you can get done in four hours a week. A block of time can help you create content in batches and help you work in advance.

If you have a bigger team, I typically recommend four hours per full-time employee. It's not a perfect science but helps you work out capacity. I haven't included time engaging with replies on social media posts which can also take time every day. (I tend to pop on and off through the day between meetings)

We give our clients a spreadsheet to help organise their social media content. You can take a look at this, and download our free daily planner sheet on **beaspiderbuildaweb.com**.

KEEP IT SUSTAINABLE

I love the new challenge of jumping into an activity. Keeping it going however, is a different story!

It's better to start at a pace you can maintain and commit yourself to, even if it is a small amount of marketing, and then, once this starts feeling automatic and easy, add on something else.

I often say, "it's better to be consistently average than sporadically brilliant". Your audience will trust you more if they keep on seeing you over time.

So often I work with business owners who'll email their list three or four times in a month, forget to get back to it for eight months, do a few more emails, then forget again.

If you're learning a new skill, break it down into simple steps to build a habit. For instance, if you're wanting to use LinkedIn, set up your profile, and then use two to three weeks to just get into the practice of logging into the app every day and connecting to others. Read a few posts and then log out.

Then for the next few weeks, begin to comment on other people's posts, then when that feels comfortable, start posting once, then twice and up to as much as every day as you get used to it. It's all about keeping it manageable and seeing growth over time.

AVOID SHINY OBJECT SYNDROME

I am a sucker for shiny objects in marketing. I have learned to take a little look at it and then ask myself "is this something that adds to my current plan?", "is this something my clients will use?", and "is this something I need right now?"

I was incredibly tempted to jump onto Clubhouse when it launched. I had an iPhone. I got an early invite. It gave you an opportunity to talk with a bunch of incredible people all over the world. It appealed to my desire to feel special and get noticed by well-known people in my industry. What more could I ask for?

To use it properly would have meant sucking up time that was best used elsewhere. My clients didn't use it and weren't interested in it. To top it all off, I realised it was my ego wanting to be on it, more than my need to serve my business. So I stepped away. Did I miss out? Maybe. But it didn't pass the test of fitting my overall strategy, so I moved past it.

STOP LOOKING AT YOUR COMPETITORS

I often remind my clients that they cannot be expected to have the same levels of output as me when doing their own marketing. I've been a content writer for over twenty years. I work as a marketer so I live and breathe marketing ideas, and I've got others in my team who help with design, some writing, and the admin of marketing.

You don't know what help others are getting to make all their marketing happen. They may have more time because they are less busy than you are, or because they're opting to sacrifice sleep.

Focus on what you are doing and stop looking over your shoulder.

RESTRICT YOUR INFORMATION SOURCES

I'm very careful to check who I follow and read online. I'm constantly learning and developing my knowledge and skills and following other marketers and writers. I make sure they have similar values to mine and check I'm following people that are recognised leaders in their space.

Often the content I read is American and needs to be Kiwified/Aussified for our specific needs. I'll spend time fact checking, or go directly to the source. I test ideas out and see if they work. I'll check in with other colleagues who have similar types of clients. I have to do this as I'm often advising our clients of updates. That is part of my "proper work".

You are going to need to stay updated too. It's important for you to get advice and help. Do remember, we can get overwhelmed by taking in too much conflicting information and not having time to work out what's the best fit for your business.

It's common to see people asking questions like "what's a great CRM?" or "how do I advertise my business?" online, and watch people kindly jumping in to answer with something that has worked for them, but might not fit the business owner who asked.

If you are going to use Facebook groups to get help and support, please take time to write a detailed breakdown of your type of business, the stage of your business, and what outcomes you need before getting answers. It's also a good idea to ask people why they'd recommend it.

If someone offers their business as a solution, choose them only if you relate to them and trust them. There are marketers out there who I find easy to relate to, and others who make me feel anxious. Guess which ones I follow and subscribe to?

I asked the people in our Facebook MAP IT Marketing group what advice they'd give to someone who felt overwhelmed by information overload. Heather Carrigan, who owns a flax floristry school, suggested choosing only one or two people at a time to learn from. You don't need to stick with them permanently, but find someone you trust and commit to just listening to them for a month, and applying their information.

PREPARE TO OUTSOURCE

Getting extra help makes marketing easier. If growing your team is part of your plan, we recommend putting aside money for help for three months before you take anyone on. Starting with a marketing virtual assistant to help with the admin side of marketing can be the lowest risk/highest reward combo to begin with. (They can post content, subtitle videos, research ideas and more).

One of the biggest mistakes we see in small businesses is they jump into outsourcing marketing before understanding how it all works first. This leaves you wide open to be sold things you don't need, or pay for marketing that doesn't reflect your business, your voice and your values. It can also mean you are looking for a solution on a small budget, which may not get you great results.

It can be painful and time consuming to learn about marketing as a small business owner.

However, as one of the core components of your business, it's part of your job, just as understanding your accounts, and looking after your customers. As you grow, you can use team members and external help to keep it all going, working up to having an inhouse marketing manager whose job is to focus on marketing alone.

PART THREE
WHO IS OUR WEB CATCHING?

CHAPTER 8

DON'T MAKE THIS MARKETER CRY

I KNOW THIS BOOK IS ALL ABOUT BUILDING A WEB, BUT LIKE ANY GREAT construction project, the end result will look better if we do a whole bunch of planning first. So before we start to build our web, we've got a little bit more work to do together.

Many people confuse actions and tactics with strategy. They think "if I learn how to use TikTok I'll be able to sell lots of my product there."

But if you don't know who you are targeting, what they want from your products, and how to get their attention best, you'll just have an account with poor video views, a couple of random comments and a smattering of followers. (Although knowing TikTok, you'll get a single video going viral for no reasonable reason, get five hundred thousand views on it, think it's going to make you TikTok famous, and still make no sales!)

A marketing strategy starts with working out exactly what you are going to sell, who exactly you are going to sell it to, and why they need it. From there, you are ready to work out where you need to be to reach those people.

That all sounds simple, but it is the hardest part of creating a marketing strategy by yourself. We are limited by our knowledge of different types of people, our bias, our mindset, our goals, how we think people should act, our desire to take short cuts, or our belief in how hard or easy it is to write, communicate or sell—and so much more.

There are some questions I always ask when I'm helping clients work out what we're going to be talking about and who we're talking to. I'm an action taker. I like getting a cool idea and jumping right in to try it out. But I know that can be the biggest waste of time if you don't have the purpose and focus behind it all.

So I'd like you to push down that desire to flick past this annoying but very necessary part of marketing and answer the following questions:

1. Who are you marketing to?
2. What are you marketing to them?
3. Why do they need it?

WHO ARE YOU MARKETING TO?

There is one sure fire way to make this marketer cry. All you have to do, when I ask you that age old question 'who is your target market?', is to answer either "everyone" OR "anyone who wants it".

Remember my story of learning to talk to one person at a time? When we're marketing, we need to remember that "if you're selling to everyone, you're selling to no one". Or "if you try to be all things to all people, you won't be anything to anybody".

The world's population has become incredibly open to us as business owners. We used to just be confined to our local region, only able to use traditional signage, maybe a branded car and a newspaper article from time to time. Big organisations with lots of money could spend thousands of dollars on corporate sponsorship and television advertising.

But all of those things changed when technology changed and allowed a business of any size and budget to get in front of their audience. With a simple website, and using social media platforms, you can talk directly to your customer. But the problem is—so can everyone else.

And with every business doing it, it creates a very noisy space. Suddenly, we are all competing against all the others who are trying to get the attention of your prospective customer.

Of course, it makes sense for you to think 'I'm going to market to everybody' because when you feel like you are marketing to everyone, it means you can say 'I'm keeping open. I'm going to allow myself to be able to talk to whoever comes my way. I am going to sell them whatever it is they want.' But there is a problem with that. If we try to market and talk to everybody, our messaging stops being directed at anyone in particular.

Combine that with all the noise of other businesses' messages and imagery going past people on a daily basis, and yours will just get lost.

When we market to a specific someone, it helps us to define the way we speak. We direct our conversation to a specific type of person. We talk about what it is they need and want. They will feel it's just for them, know we understand them and know what it is they are looking for.

Which takes me back to the first part of this section. Please don't ever tell a marketer you're marketing to everyone. Whole books have been written about this topic but it seems to be the part business owners really struggle with. Perhaps it's boring, or too 'scary' to think about narrowing your target audience, but it must be done. We have an innate desire to add numerous exceptions to our ideal customer profile JUST IN CASE.

On **beaspiderbuildaweb.com** there is a simple worksheet that can help you with the process, but the easiest place to start is to think about who they are. You might want to define them as a personality, or as an individual person with a name, especially if you have a B2C business (business to consumer).

CHAPTER 9

YOU NEED TO NARROW YOUR ARROW

It's best you know that, if your life depended on it, you should not ask me to pick up a physical bow and arrow to defend you. No matter how sharp and pointy that arrowhead is, I'm not going to get it anywhere near the spot I'm trying to target.

However, if we're talking metaphorical arrows in your marketing, I'm your warrior woman! I can take that old blunt, wide arrowhead, and carve it down to a focussed pointy weapon that will pierce through that wall of success you've been wanting to get through for years.

If you want better leads and more sales with your ideal target audience you need to narrow the arrow.

(Before I go on, I have to admit I stole the phrase from someone during one of my training sessions. They came up with it, I loved it and immediately said I'd be using it forevermore. I am thankful she gave me permission. I did forget to note her name so if that's you, THANK YOU!)

WHAT DOES NARROW THE ARROW MEAN?

Imagine that before you is a wall. Behind that wall is all the success and growth you seek. Your job is to push through it with an arrow.

If your arrow is blunt or wide, it's not going to punch through. You're going to need a narrow, pointy arrow.

A narrow pointy arrow in your business is one that is very targeted. It's got no room for waste. It's clearly here for business, and it's going to get it.

Our marketing arrows can become blunted wide arrows. We want it to reach as many people in one shot as possible. We want them to know everything at once. We feel we've got to stuff the arrowhead with a whole bunch of offers, opportunities.

We stop thinking about that arrow as targeting a specific sort of prey (We don't want to kill them. It's a nice arrow. Promise.) But—the more we weigh down that arrowhead and stuff it with everything, the slower and more cumbersome it gets. The blunter the tip becomes. The harder it becomes for it to pick up speed and maintain momentum.

That wall of success gets harder to penetrate.

We narrow our arrows when we refine what we sell, and who we sell it to. The more we narrow, the more targeted we can be in our marketing.

It takes bravery to reduce and refine, to unpack that broad arrowhead and carve it back to a sharp and pointy weapon. It's scary to watch the additions and extras you popped on to make yourself look bigger, more open, more "better for everyone just in case" lying there discarded on the floor. It's scary to trust that the targeted arrow is going to find its mark.

You can keep all that you drop in a safe place. You can come back to it, and fashion new arrows from those bits and pieces. But first, you've got to push through that initial wall of success.

To do that you've got to narrow that arrow. Make it pointy and sharp. And know exactly what it's targeting.

YOU'VE GOT TO NARROW WHO YOU TARGET

You may have heard of the "customer avatar" or "target persona" or "target market".

Large businesses spend thousands developing a very specific type of customer avatar. I was trained to do this too when I learned how to become a marketing strategist.

A customer avatar might like a bit like this:

Carol is a 32 year old professional in financial services who lives in a large urban centre. She commutes to work each day and uses that time to listen to blogs about parenting, investing and true crime.

Carol is on a 100k salary, and is trying to buy her first home with her partner Michael. They are also talking about staying healthy and are trying to cut down the amount of takeaways they are eating each week.

Carol loves to cook but just doesn't have time to plan her meals each week. She's looking for simple ways to get her meal prep sorted and organised so all she has to do is cook it all up quickly at the end of the day (and hopefully make a great lunch for the next day too).

Any guesses what this would be an avatar for?

If you guessed a weekly grocery and menu delivery service you've got it in one!

I DON'T RATE CUSTOMER AVATARS FOR MOST SMALL BUSINESS OWNERS

This may be my one-way ticket to being kicked out of all self-respecting marketing circles (I suspect I'm already out regardless!) but I'm not a fan of the work so many strategists and marketers do around customer avatars for small business owners.

I often have to undo the trauma of small business owners who've gone to a workshop and told to create a "person" that's their exact demographic. It's not that it doesn't have its place, but often the end result is something so specific you've narrowed your target market to an audience of three.

Sometimes I read the description of the person and it's either a carbon copy of the business owner (and you don't need you, because you've already got you), or it's filled with so many pain points and deep issues that all you're going to attract is a neurotic client who will cause you more pain than you were hoping to fix in their life.

Customer avatars started in big corporate America, where the target market is around a million people, and the companies producing them could afford to spend time, money, and research working out who was the best fit for their product or service.

Even with all this work, it wasn't a foolproof method for getting it right. What people say in a focus group, or for us, a Facebook group, needs to be taken with a grain of salt. For every fifty people who tell you it's something they'd love, it's likely there is one of them who'll actually pay for it when it's released.

Most business owners do not have the capacity, or the budget to create a proper custom avatar, and it's often not required. If you're the only yoga teacher with a Facebook page in your local area, if you are an engineering firm with a speciality in a specific area, or you've got a strong personality that people have got to like if they're going to work with you, a traditional customer avatar is not what you need.

If you've got worldwide domination in mind, and the money to back it, then taking time to create a customer avatar makes a lot of sense. It will help you connect with your people out of the billions of people on this planet, and it's worth the investment.

However, for many of us, a full-blown customer avatar is overkill. It may even make your target market too small. Last year, I worked with a woman who wanted to work with a specific avatar. She'd come to me with a very clear target persona. I took it, and we created a strategy around her ideal client. They were price sensitive so she had to price her offer at a rate that meant she had to get large numbers of people using her solution. Something didn't feel right. On investigation, the target market and the offer didn't work together. There were only five hundred people who fit her ideal client profile in the whole country. We had to make her narrow arrow a little wider to make success possible.

Let's take another look at the client avatar of Carol. It's the layers behind it we need to focus on.

Carol, the ideal client has the following attributes:

1. She lives in a big city
2. She has a professional job and a six-figure salary
3. She spends a lot of time in traffic
4. She's budget conscious
5. She is time poor
6. She wants to eat healthy.

If you look at your favourite clients, you may be able to pull out some common problems they might need you to solve. When we look at the above list, you'll see the first three points are describing her lifestyle, and the last three show three areas that you can help with your solution (if you are a food box subscription service.)

As I mentioned before, my training in digital marketing came from a group of American marketers who define the ideal size for a target group to be around the one million mark. This number could be smaller for a business who has a premium market, and little need for large numbers of clients, but it certainly puts many of our options into perspective.

In New Zealand, for instance, with a population of five million, that's a big catchment space! And for all the businesses I've worked with in small towns, or regional areas, that is a far bigger market than they can accommodate. Especially if they are marketing within a specific geographical area.

SEVEN WAYS TO IDENTIFY YOUR IDEAL CUSTOMER

Identifying the main reasons someone might need what you sell is the first step in working out how to narrow the arrow of who you are targeting. But it's not the only thing you can use.

I've found working through the following seven areas, discarding the ones that don't fit you, selecting two or three that fit best, and using these to create a focus can help you know exactly who you are aiming to reach and convert to a customer.

1. Pinpoint an industry

You can target people working in specific industries. You might choose to only work with accountants, or hairdressers, engineers or people in ecommerce. It might be a whole group of people who have a particular type of job and that's who you want to work with. I would recommend having two industries, just to protect yourself. A few businesses I've worked with focussed on a single industry, such as tourism, and really struggled during Covid-19 because all of their eggs were in that basket.

2. Feed their desire

Retail is built on feeding desire. I'm a sneaker wearer—it's pretty much all I wear. I could get away with owning maybe three pairs of sneakers, one for walking/working out, and two for work. I have currently got FIFTEEN pairs. I'm currently eying up a couple of other pairs. I'm open to sneaker temptation, and those sneaky shoe businesses on the internet keep on showing me their soft leather, bouncy sole offers and all I want is them.

You can narrow down by desire. What is it that that person wants? Could it be they want shoes or they do want beautiful clothing or jewellery? You need to evoke a desire to help them have those things. This is a perfect fit for businesses that sell consumer goods, where you are attracting people who want to have those needs fulfilled.

3. Solve a problem

This is a traditional part of creating a customer avatar. One of the questions you can ask is "What keeps your ideal customer up at night?"

It might be literal (the snoring next to you, the two-year-old who can't settle), or a little more philosophical. There is something about that 3 a.m. terror loop knowing you've got to fix that bad habit, the financial mess you've slidden into, or how to mend a relationship.

While you don't want to poke the bruise sadistically, you do want to remind them of it in daylight enough to then lead them to your solution.

The crucial part of this is getting the problem that they want solved correct. Part of the issue is that humans often confuse the messages between want and need. What we think we need is often what we just desire. When targeting a problem, it needs to be the problem your ideal customer identifies, which might be different from the problem you know they have.

The pain of the problem has to be big enough and hard enough to solve. They know they need someone else to help step in and fix it. You will need to pinpoint what that problem is and then show how you are going to solve it.

4. Attract with your values

We talked about the need for identifying your values right at the beginning of this book. When we share our values in our marketing, they will either resonate with others or turn them off.

People are attracted to our values either because they are similar to theirs or they are aspirational values they want to have. If you are building a personal brand or a brand with a strong values base, targeting people by sharing your values can help to attract people who are similar to you. Because you share that with others, you end up meeting and interacting with those who value those same things.

For example, if you have a social enterprise, or focus on a sustainable brand, naming the values you'd expect your ideal client to have makes it easier to create marketing collateral that attracts them.

5. Pinpoint a location

One of the simplest ways to narrow your arrow is to specify a geographical area. If you live in a town or service an area of less than one hundred thousand people, it's likely that's a good-sized audience to focus on. You then just need to add one other element and you are sorted. Local businesses often minimise the importance of focussing on their location area. Your location can be bigger, such as a state, country, or region, but you'd need to use several other factors to make the ideal group of your ideal people smaller.

6. Build a personal stage

If your product or service requires people to have a high level of trust in you, having a very clear individual personal brand aligned to the business can help you do just that.

If you've got a service-based business delivering training, coaching or strategy, and are a solopreneur, it's likely this will be part of your narrow arrow target market. However, it can work with any type of business.

As you show your face via photos and video, share your ideas and communication style, and make the brand synonymous with yourself, people will either be drawn to your business, or be repelled away from it.

This type of narrowing works best if you're targeting a large population catchment. If you've got a strong personality attached to a brand, looking after a town of fifteen thousand, and there are little to no competitors, it may lead someone to drive forty-five minutes to find another option!

Our business made the conscious decision to focus on personality after we defined our values. While we have all sorts of personalities in the business, my style is what we use to attract the right people to our business.

For trust to work, you need to like and know the person first. As a trust-based business, this is one of the simplest methods to build that trust, as people will follow you, listen to you and refer to you if they like you and the things you say.

7. Ride the trend wave

If you're an early adopter, a trend sniffer, or powerful enough to create your own trend (you'll also have used personality to make that happen), this could be the one you've been looking for.

You could become the expert in a new type of social media. I've watched people build entire businesses on how to create reels, or becoming a Clubhouse[1] expert. Both of those appeared at about the same time, and while Reels remain a high interest topic (and the time of writing), the other, Clubhouse, has all but died a death.

Trends, if you get them right, come with huge opportunities. Trends if you get them wrong, can come with sunk costs and little to show for them. This is how we end up with clearance sales on Tamagotchis and Fidget Spinners. They were bought in bulk by people who caught the wave too late.

If you love watching the wave of new, have an uncanny eye to spot the new obsessions and know how to move fast, targeting trends is a perfect fit for you. The key is to be hunting for the next trend, before the current trend dives.

Choose one, two or three. This is your blend of perfect.

To create your idea persona, you need to get blending.

Take these seven areas and choose one, two or three to create the ideal client profile. You could just choose one. You can say 'I am going to target everyone in a 5km radius from my house', narrowing down on location. Or you might say 'I am going to target everyone in a 5km radius around my house who needs to get their haircut.' And that is narrowing on location and their problem. Or then you could say 'I am going to target everyone in a 5km radius who needs a haircut, but also likes that I have a high level of expertise in cutting curly hair.' Which might be around meeting the desire of someone to have a really professional hair style.

Go through them, modify them, and create your profile. You don't want to have more than three elements. While we're focussing on local businesses, it's also a good idea to do a brief check on competitors, and see what message they are using. Two hairdressers talking about offering an experience for curly haired folk, or "going blonde" in the same area becomes a war of who can say it loudest. If someone is already owning that space locally, it's often better to find another focus. People will still know you've got all the expertise, once they come to you.

NARROWING THE ARROW ISN'T EXCLUDING OTHERS

A common concern from business owners going through this process is "But if I stop telling people everything I do, surely I'll leave people out, and my business will be less successful."

It's an understandable fear. It doesn't make sense that to become more successful we have to limit our audience.

When we define our target audience by industry or professional body and then target a specific need or niche—like period products for teens, or industrial tools for engineers—something that really narrows it down to a particular market, we help make it easier for people looking to meet a specific need to pay attention. The world out there has become very noisy and we're all walking around in a permanent space of distraction, so we're finding the simplest method to help your message stay focussed, repeatable and clear to meet a specific target.

It doesn't mean we're being exclusionary however. We want to ensure you can get the attention of that group of people, but also not be so narrow that there are not enough people in that market to come along.

What happens if your market is a particular fit, and then someone comes along who is outside it? Well, you're not going to say to them 'sorry, please go away because you are not my target market'. Of course you're still going to allow them to come in your door because obviously they have been attracted to what you do and what you sell, and they have made the decision to work with you—and that is totally fine. But what this is all about is using the target market to get the right message in front of the BEST people for your business. It helps us to get clarity on who this is, and also enables us to make our marketing messaging much simpler and more straightforward, because we're not trying to appeal to a wide range of people.

So please don't make me cry. You need to have a think about who exactly it is you are marketing to before we create a web to catch them and continue to talk as they journey down the decision Hub. Write it down, describe them, what their needs might be and why they might want to buy from you.

CHAPTER 10

IT'S A NEED-TO-KNOW BASIS

YEARS AGO, I WAS WORKING WITH A BUSINESS OWNER (WE'LL CALL HIM Sam) who lived in a small town. He ran an IT support business, and he was deeply unhappy about it.

The business had an admirable turnover. And Sam had a steady stream of customers. But it was missing two really important elements for a small business.

First, while it had a good turn over, it wasn't very profitable. The business mainly did work that was, by its very nature, low margin busy work. Secondly, this sort of work was stuff he didn't like to do. Sam felt trapped and had no idea how to resolve it.

We managed to get him his joy back (because who wants to be in a business that makes you miserable. We also helped him make more money). I'm going to explain what we did, but first it's worth talking about how he got into this problem in the first place, as the accidental journey to business despair is all too common.

When Sam started his business, he offered the services he really wanted to do. His joy was going into businesses and helping them with working out what computer and IT systems they'd need, and then installing these. He wanted to become their tech guy if any issues came up. He had big plans, and the town he lived in was big enough to support them.

While he grew, Sam started to take on little bits of work, offering simple IT fixes to anyone who needed them. The investigation of the problem often took far more time than people would pay, so he started to trim off the actual time he was taking to make it feel more palatable.

Sam found that flat rate offers were far more appealing to these little customers, and they were also easier for him on an accounting basis. So he created a deal, and because his work with the bigger clients was still building and he had capacity, he created an advertisement to get more of these deals. He changed the messaging on his website. He made signs in his workshop and started to talk about the cheap offer to everyone to attract more of these little customers.

In his head, he was creating a short-term fix. In reality he created a long-term problem.

I met Sam four years after he'd made that call. He wasn't working with any of the businesses he'd set up to serve. Instead, his days were filled up to bursting with low paid, stressful, busy work. He wanted to change, he was trying to change, and he couldn't understand why he wasn't getting the right customers.

The first misstep was living in the panic of "doing things in the meantime." I've done it myself. When you hit a little dry spell it's easy to panic, and think, "I'll just take this little bit of work on to keep me covered."

Sometimes we do need to do something for survival, but we need to keep it TOP SECRET.

Don't be tempted to make it a regular offer. Don't add it onto your website as a service. And don't make all your testimonials come from people you've done this work for.

WHAT YOU SOW YOU GROW

Sam unintentionally grew a business from the wrong seeds. When I went on his website, it was all about his special offers. His reviews on Google were also for the same sort of work, and his social media posts mainly covered this work too.

Somewhere between "I'll just take this to tide me over " and "I've got a business I hate" there were many little slips into changing his focus publicly. He was known as a fix-it guy locally, and because this took up all his time, he couldn't get the work he really wanted. He had to keep pushing the low value work to keep the cash flow going.

Sometimes the crop you've produced is completely wrong. And it's like a weed, suffocating your core product or services. It will not allow you to grow the way you planned.

STEEL YOURSELF FOR LOSSES BEFORE GAINS

If you've accidentally built the wrong type of business you've got some choices to make.

The first is to just suck it up, keep on eating from a harvest of undesirable planting (akin to my middle child having to eat endless capsicum!). The benefit is that you don't need to change anything. Sometimes we have seasons where we're not ready to change, perhaps because everything else around us is a hurricane.

Sometimes we've built something that will cost too much to change. I worked with a woman with a tooth whitening business who knew she had to change her model, but could not afford the inevitable short term drop of income while her business reset itself.

It's a terrible position to be in, but it's a valid reason to stay the same.

If you know you need to change, you will need to go through some discomfort first.

SLOWLY CLAW BACK SOME SPACE

Unless you've got a nest egg, or are otherwise supported, the safest way is to clear space in your planting for the thing you really want to do. Decide to clear a day a week, and ban yourself from doing any work other than working on your ideal offer.

On paper this sounds super simple, but the reality is that it's a behaviour and mindset shift. It's very easy to block the day out. It's one thing entirely to make the day just for your preferred line of work!

When I realised that no one actually knows what's on my calendar, and that as a business owner, I get to decide what I'm working on any given day, it became easier. I do not need to give excuses or explain how I run my time and neither do you.

If you can afford more time, take it. If you can't, then start with a half day. Make it really worth your time. Look at using this time to change your messaging step by step. Block out time for specific tasks and chip away at replanting your new crop.

BURN THE FIELDS

If you've got a nest egg, or you've got support to help tide you over during a low earning period, then the other option is to burn down everything you are doing now (this is not a literal suggestion to burn your office!). You then replant, fertilise and focus completely on your ideal offer.

Sometimes you don't even need to have a nest egg.

We needed to make huge changes to our offer. Our business was already losing money. By burning down the old offers, removing them from our website, and saying no to all future work that didn't fit our ideal work, we both had more time to focus on the right type of work, and we lost less money.

If you're going to do this, you'll still need to complete any work you've currently got on offer and it's a good idea to hunt around and find someone else who can take your old, 'valued but not a great fit' clients so they remain supported and don't hate you forever for dumping them. (No one likes a messy break up!)

This is the option Sam took. He was even able to make a little on the deal, selling his list of customers to a local business who loved doing what he hated. He carefully managed his transition, explained to his customer base that he was only going to focus on working with companies to solve their IT systems and he was away.

He also managed to pick up two clients during this transition. Several of his customers had no idea that he could work on bigger projects. They recommended him to the decision maker at their work, and within a few weeks he was in bliss working on two large projects.

Not everyone gets a lucky catch that fast, but often the very action of closing a door with purpose and announcing another door is opening up can lead to new ideal work from your existing community.

CHAPTER 11

YOU'VE GOT TO NARROW YOUR OFFER

Once we've narrowed our audience, we need to narrow what we're going to sell

You don't want to end up like Sam and have a business that's busy with unfulfilling and unprofitable work, so you get to be a little self-indulgent here.

We're going to work on you growing a business in areas you have a long-term interest in, that keeps you captivated and interested enough to get through the hard bits, and laser focussed on several core services, or products.

There is a certain magic in a store that sells everything. It's also an incredibly distracting place to visit. You go in with a shopping list of three items you need, and come out forty-five minutes later with a shopping trolley filled with everything but the three items you went in for.

We used to have a business like this. I started off offering social media management (which in itself was disastrous as I got bored writing captions, and sourcing images after six weeks. It was only a matter of time my clients and my bank account were going to be disappointed). Then people wanted branding, websites, strategy, ads, Adwords, and logos. They wanted everything marketing all under one roof.

I didn't want to say no to the opportunity. I just kept on saying yes.

I had to grow a team to accommodate all the different options, and now had extra mouths to feed. A lot of the work was out of my own skill set. I had to keep selling all of these services so I could keep paying for my team.

I grew a big business, a busy business, a broken business and a business I didn't really love, all wrapped up in a big pile of "offering everything to anyone."

Our website was sixty-five pages of offers, with long pages of descriptions of all the cool things we did. When people visited our site, they stayed for an average of eight minutes.

They also rarely got in contact.

We'd made an "everything store" business, and all we'd really built was a generalist shop where people browsed then bounced off to go find a specialist. We needed to narrow the arrow on our offer.

When we hit the wall and realised we needed to change, one of the turning points was sitting down and asking ourselves the following questions:

- What are we really good at?
- What do we make money on?
- What do we lose money on?
- What do we love doing?
- What do we not enjoy?
- What's dependent on us having to "feed" a staff with new work consistently to keep them busy, and us profitable?
- What can we do with a small team?
- What do we want to be known for?
- What skills do us as business owners have that will always be around?
- What can we see people really need?
- What work attracted our best customers?
- What work attracted our worst?

- What do I (as a person and business owner) want to be doing more of?
- What do I want to do less of or drop completely?

We got out big pieces of paper, we used big markers and post it notes (because these make difficult meetings more fun) and we answered these questions as business owners.

I turned off my little trigger-happy solution buttons, and I went through this full process with an open mind. Some of these questions felt almost too self-indulgent to answer. What do you mean I could ask myself what sort of business I wanted? Was I allowed to think about how that business would be in relation to the rest of my life?

Once through, the end result was very clear. Our marketing strategies and training gave us the most joy, fitted in with our goals, made money, and was something I could do myself.

We also had a small range of other activities we knew we also wanted and needed to offer. We kept these but didn't make these a focus in our marketing. We decided to only offer these to people who'd already come in the "marketing strategy" door.

This didn't immediately fix our business, but the impact of narrowing our offer was almost immediate. We changed our message everywhere, cut out all the noise and excess information on our website, and made it very difficult for anyone to get distracted from our core message: "We help small business owners write a marketing strategy and action plan".

The leads and enquiries started to come in. We narrowed the arrow of our offer, and we broke through the wall to success.

WHAT ABOUT RETAIL?

Can this work for retail the same way? Most definitely.

It might be that the range within your "narrow" offer is broad in terms of styles, or colours.

The key is to find the thing you want to be known for. Is it brightly coloured party dresses? High quality cookware? The best quality sustainable natural skincare?

Narrowing your offer is not about being limited in what you sell. It's about focussing on a simple message that attracts your ideal client, and then opens the door to sell them your other things once they've walked on through.

Trying to create a memorable message that squeezes every item you sell onto your social media and website front page just leaves you feeling anxious and overwhelmed, and your customer indecisive and ready to go find a simpler offer.

NARROWING YOUR OFFER BUILDS A NETWORK

One of the best ways to grow your business is through strategic alliances with other similar or complementary businesses that can refer to you, and vice versa. An unexpected benefit of narrowing what we did and who we would work with was it helped us work better with other businesses. These same businesses were ones I'd viewed as competitors only a few months before.

There is something very refreshing in saying no to a prospective customer and then giving them a better solution, because what they aren't isn't something you do best, or sell.

You benefit because you've stuck to your focus, the customer thinks you are cool for helping them, and you've built a deeper relationship with another business owner. The customer benefits because they still get what they need. And the other business owner benefits from the extra business. It's a triple shot of awesome.

CHAPTER 12

A MASERATI FOR $4.99

THE END GOAL IS PROFIT.

That's going to feel jarring to you if you've got money mindset issues. I was raised in a home where money was appreciated, but it wasn't polite to talk about it. My memories of a lot of my (predominantly happy) childhood are laced with anxious conversations about what we could and couldn't afford. I felt resentful when my mother wouldn't buy me new school blouses after my body developed, seemingly overnight, and my shirt gaped. This much to the delight of the fifteen boys in my class who used to line themselves up to peek between the gaps as I tried to work at my desk. It wasn't so delightful to me.

Now that I have experienced the tension of knowing there are things that must be bought, yet know there are bigger things to buy, I get it. I had a terrible relationship with money for a long time. After never having a lot, when I got some, I wasted it. I was very good at making it. Not so good at keeping it. As a single mother we had months where we went out to brunch every Saturday, and others where I worried the power would be cut off.

When I'm speaking to a business owner about marketing, we always spend time talking about profit. No matter what your long-term intention for the business is, no matter how noble the cause, it needs profit for it to pay you, be healthy, stable and continue to grow.

Last week I was working with a client and working on mindset

And I used this phrase "You do not have the right to decide if your customer can afford you or not. That is their decision"

And then I realised,

I do it all the time. And it needs to stop.

We have people who can easily afford us baulk at our prices because we are "too expensive"

And others I think are too small make a call to pay the money because they understand the value

It's not our job to make our offer smaller, (or even try to make something to squeeze into their small budget) or not present it to someone who asks because we feel it's not the right time.

If they see value, if they trust us, if they want it, they'll get it. Your offer is your offer. Presenting it the best way you can is your job

Them choosing it is theirs

(And if you don't give them that opportunity, they will need to go somewhere else and not get you)

Yes. It's a funny thing, that word profit. A lot of people don't like talking about it.

We might want to have a certain lifestyle, dream of our own homes, regular holidays, not having to stress about paying for groceries, or getting our bills paid, or being able to do crazy things like buying a brand-new car with cash, or just never lying awake worrying about money.

We're all at different stages of money mindset, and a chapter in a book about marketing is unlikely to shift you dramatically, but I can tell you that your business growth will be limited by the mindset you have around money.

Here's some broken record mantras I've heard myself or my clients say over the years:

- "I'm terrible with money"
- "There's never enough"
- "I can't put my prices up because then I'll be too expensive"
- "I wouldn't pay that amount for that"
- "I want to make it cheap enough so everyone can afford it"
- "I'm worried people will think I'm arrogant if I price at that value"
- "I'm reinvesting everything back into the business now, but it's going to pay off (at a time that rarely comes)
- "My business is about creating impact, so I'm not really worried about profit"
- "I'm going through a growth period, so it's normal for the business to not make money over this (unending) time."

It's a really good idea to take time to sit and reflect about what lies you tell yourself about money.

I'm always devastated when a business owner, who's working sixty-plus hours a week in their business tells me their goals for the business, and it includes one day being able to pay themselves minimum wage.

At the very least, your business should pay you the market rates of what you'd need to pay someone else to do your job in your business. Plus, a percentage of profit as director drawings for the benefit of owning a business, and carrying the extra responsibilities that brings. Ok?

WORK OUT WHERE YOU FIT

Part of working out your message includes working out where you fit in your niche, in terms of offer. This will be reflected in your pricing.

If you're offering premium coaching for forty dollars an hour, it's not going to be trusted.

Similarly if you offer a cut rate group coaching option for two thousand a month, the one-to-one coaching better be REALLY GOOD.

A cheap fry pan will get a lot of angry reviews if you price it up there with the premium quality pans, then the non-stick surface degrades after a couple of goes. And while a cast iron pan is a steal for under fifty dollars, your target market is not going to trust it at that price.

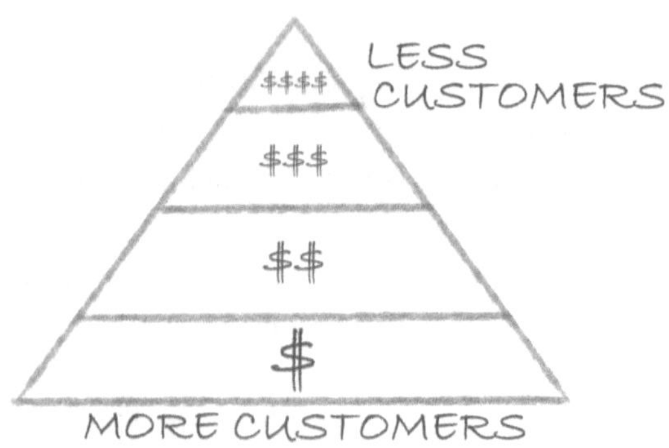

If there's one thing I've learned from working with hundreds of small business owners, it's that a large percentage of us do not value what we do enough to make sure we're getting paid for all our hard work. We definitely pay our team, our suppliers, and we're all about the great deals for our customers… But when it comes to us? We come last.

When I started my business Identify, I priced everything as if I was still a freelancer. (And a cheap one at that.) I had no idea of how to ensure all my business costs were covered. When Identify grew, and I had to pay people every week (which I did no matter what), I found the business could no longer pay me. Plus, I was "reinvesting" any extras I did have back into the business.

These are very common traps I see my own clients fall into over and over again. As business owners we often see our salary is some sort of reward for getting to a random destination of success. We focus on a huge future payday as our carrot that's always there in front of us, but never quite in reach. Over time, that carrot starts to get smaller and smaller, as our mindset shifts and we stop being able to visualise the success we started out so sure we'd get to.

Our business needs to be built to include the cost of paying ourselves into the pricing right from the beginning. It's the only way we can build a business that can both pay us from the start, and grow bigger.

BREAK THE CYCLE

As you'll see, I've had to do a lot of work around pricing and mindset. It's difficult to break cycles of behaviour that go on autopilot. It's difficult to see beyond your own understanding.

Even now my brain has limits. I'm all good with the goals we have, but I'm unable to visualise "I'm just going to pop down to the helicopter pad to ask the pilot to go pick up dinner" wealthy.

Knowing where we sit, and how we've been conditioned by circumstance, by the people around us, and our current state, can help us see if that view is having an impact on how we price, and sell our services.

There are many reasons we have a block around pricing. Below are some of the more common ones. If you know you struggle to price yourself correctly, perhaps it's because of one of the following.[1]

MINDSET MATTERS

The start-up culture has a lot to answer for, for most "normal" businesses.

We have all heard the stories of people with a dream, starting out in their garages, working for years late into the night with nothing but a part time job at a supermarket, and the love of their parents to keep them from dying of starvation.

Start-up culture is about that big payday, when an investor helps your dreams become reality, or perhaps even buys you out for millions.

Meanwhile you've scraped buy, given away shares as payment, and hoped your idea is the one.

We hear the success stories but the percentage of these compared to the failures is minimal.

Many b usiness owners have embraced the start-up success dream, and fall into the trap of needing to sacrifice everything to see success (which I call profit.)

It's even worse if we are doing work we love to do. It can feel wrong to charge a premium for work we actually enjoy. Positively sinful. We believe we need to suffer, so we don't try to find a different way that sees us profitable from the start.

WE FORGET ABOUT US

Yesterday I was asking a new client if they paid themselves in the business. They said yes. So I asked them "The amount you're paying yourself, is it the same or more than it would cost to replace you doing that work?", and then I went for the second jab: "And are you also taking a profit payment on top for being the business owner?"

The answer to both of these questions was an uncomfortable silence.

As business owners we are often the lowest paid people in our business, even if we're doing the same work as a staff member. Imagine if you offered someone else the money you're paying yourself? What would they say?

This issue starts the moment we set our pricing. We need to factor in the hours in the work, the hours doing all the "other" work, our "owner's reward", and a little more for growing the business.

WE'RE EATING BURNT TOAST

The official name for this is "Burnt Chop Syndrome". I like to call it burnt toast, because it reminds me of every time I took the piece of burnt toast one of my girls had discarded, and swapped it out for my perfect toast, so I could make their life easier. I'd tend to eat that toast cold, with barely warm tea. The fact I now prefer tepid tea shows how committed I was to saving my children from disappointing food experiences!

While anyone can suffer from it, it's a more common problem for parents who cook the dinner, and always take the burnt chop, the broken piece of quiche, less of the chicken, because we're putting everyone else first. We come to a business space and use the same philosophy, putting the needs of our clients, suppliers and team first without making sure we're looking after ourselves. Because we've been raised and rewarded for putting ourselves last in our personal lives, we often take this idea into our business life.

I've lost count of the times clients have told me they're the lowest paid people in their business. I was once the lowest paid person. I'd give my team pay rises, while living on nothing.

While I still have to stop myself when dishing up the chops at home, I'm no longer a follower of the "My needs come last" beliefs.

(As an aside: If I try to take the burnt chop at home, I now get lectures from my husband, and my grown children. It's really not worth attempting no matter how I feel!)

PEOPLE IN GLASSHOUSES

One of my very favourite movies of all time is *The Princess Bride*. I've lost count of how many times I've watched it. There is a scene where Princess Rosalind is dreaming of her upcoming marriage to a king she despises. As she walks down the aisle, an old woman turns, points her wizened finger at Rosalind and screams "LIAR!"

Who are we to want to earn money for this thing we do and do so well? How can we charge for this and ask for what we are worth? Maybe someone will not believe we can do this work and call us out for the FAKE that we are. It's common to be worried that our pricing will make us a target, and people will try to bring us down for owning what we do best, and pricing it for what it gives other people.

TAKE TIME TO GET IT RIGHT

Working out the correct pricing structure is an important first step in growing a successful business. I know as a marketing strategist, our first priority is making sure that any marketing we help you turn on isn't going to break your business by making it just busier and broker.

Often our clients are resistant to share pricing models and margins with us. We're looking for areas that are the best to grow, the ones that need to be adjusted, and what needs to be completely reworked before we tell people all about them.

Often the way you've worked out your pricing can be the problem. Last year I worked with a product-based business owner who had not worked out the true cost price of her product. She was selling it at just below the cost price, with no profit margin added, and was slowly destroying her business. All the marketing had to halt while we got the structure right.

WE'RE ALL BLACK BOXES

We're an assumptive lot, us humans. And we love reading between the lines of perfectly curated Instagram posts, well laid out websites, and that signwritten new car, and make judgements on just how well our competitor is doing. If there is one thing I've learned from working with thousands of small businesses on their marketing, and asking them questions about their financials, I can tell you that those outward appearances tell you nothing about the state of their business.

I've worked with a business where the business owner was about to lose her home. Her business was haemorrhaging money, and she turned up to our appointment in a huge late model car, which matched her husband's. Her social media was filled with success stories, wins and awards. And the business was about to fold.

I've also worked with a business owner who turned up in an old car, completely grubby in a ripped shirt, with barely any social media presence at all, and discovered his business was completely winning when it came to sales, and more importantly, profit.

We make so many judgements around what others are doing, but unless you're able to really look under the hood and see, that is all it is - a judgement. It's not necessarily the truth. Before you decide to set your pricing against a competitor, because it looks like it's working for them, remember, you don't know if it really is. You don't know if they have the same costs you do, if they are doing the work to the same standard or level, or if in fact it's exactly the same offer, or product.

PRICING BY THE HOUR

If you're a solopreneur, or a maker, part of your working out is considering your hourly rate and factoring this into the pricing. This is a good place to start, to check the value is at least covering this cost. This is where I started when I began Identify. The problem with this is that as you add on team members, offices and other business costs, you can lose margin or start to lose money completely.

My hourly rate was so low that I had to pay my team peanuts, and even then I was losing money. I hadn't factored tax, growth, or business costs, holidays or anything else into my rate. I couldn't pay them more, and I wasn't paying myself either! Not a great business model at all.

PRICE FOR YOUR GOALS

One of the hardest parts of business is to make clear goals that are both stretchy enough to add challenge to your current state and are achievable.

When looking at your profit goals, you need to start by working out your true costs, including what it's going to take to pay yourself market rates, and also take profit from the business. Asking yourself where you want the business to be in the future helps you create income and profit goals you want to reach. Be brave while you do this, as it's likely that the end result is something you aren't reaching right now. However now you've got an end destination to aim for.

The next step is to set some targets to help get you there. It's really important that you don't get stuck on turnover, but you focus on what the growth means for you in terms of your goals, your life and how you are creating a healthy business.

The goal is to create a healthy business that generates a consistent profit.

I recommend resetting this once a year. My mindset is able to grasp bigger numbers and is constantly evolving. The goals and vision I had for my business three years ago is tiny to the one I have today. You are allowed to increase prices, redevelop your offers, remodel the structure of your business, cut unessential costs, and make your business more profitable every year.

SETTING YOUR PRICE ON VALUE

I have a photo on my phone of a pair of Gucci tights that were once on sale. To the unfashionable eye (mine) they look like ripped pantyhose. But to a fan of Gucci they are a must have. The price listed? $190 USD.

People often think that setting your pricing on value is only for service-based businesses. Or for particular types of businesses.

In truth pricing is part of a story around the value of what you sell, to a market who can see that value and pay it. You will always be too expensive to someone, and too cheap for someone else.

We've lost on proposals for being too expensive for large businesses, and then a micro business owner has seen value in what we do and paid the same price. We've had a business owner turn us down because our pricing made us look less than the other quote that was twice the price.

Likewise, I have a dress in my wardrobe I bought for eighteen dollars, alongside one that was two hundred and another that was over six hundred. I saw value in each one of those.

Yes, if the price is high I expect more of what I buy. The quality needs to match. While I'm personally not brand driven, for some owning something from a treasured brand is enough. I once flatted with a guy who only wore Versace. He was also pretty broke, so could only afford one pair of jeans. He preferred one pair of that iconic brand, rather than buying a couple pairs of Levis and keeping the change.

You can set your pricing at whatever point you want to, as long as you can build a brand story around it that's strong enough to attract people who will pay for it. Be brave. Value your knowledge, your product and set your pricing.

CHAPTER 13

PUTTING IT ALL TOGETHER

Marketing is about telling a story.

Scrap that.

Marketing is about telling many stories that layer over each other, weaving in and out the same messages over and over again so that everyone gets a chance to hear, watch, and understand exactly why you are the right business for them.

So once we've set an audience, an offer and price positioning, we need to use these to create the web lines of your stories: Your core messages.

NARROW WHAT YOU SAY

While we can get super fancy with this, and create catch phrases, rhyming couplets and the odd rap, the best way to work out what you're going to say is to start with the following sentence starters:

"I help"

"We supply"

"We teach"

"We show"

Write a series of sentences that start with one of these, and then circle 4–5 that you can use as a framework for your message.

Make sure it is talking about one of your narrow offers and identifies your ideal customer.

For instance:

I help small business owners stay on track with their finances

We supply comfortable activewear for breastfeeding women

We teach beginner marketers how to use video confidently

We show Gen Zs the best life hacks for adulting

AVOID THIS ROOKIE MISTAKE

While you might be lucky and find one of these works perfectly as a bio on your social media pages, the biggest mistake I see business owners make at this point is keeping these statements as is, and using them ad nauseum to attract their ideal customers.

You don't have to go outright and start the obvious to show what you want.

This is why we have images, storytelling, and information our target market will want to see to help attract our ideal clients.

You don't need to add "calling all hippie mamas who love natural cleaning products" at the beginning of every post if you're selling vegan cleaning products. It's better to THINK ABOUT your ideal customers and then write your post to them without feeling you've got to call them out on every single social media post.

I recently worked with a business where we hid the core message under imagery and conversations. The public message was "Making your gut feel great." The private core message was "We help mothers who struggle with food intolerances and digestion regain their energy through gut friendly products."

TRY THEM OUT

We might not have budgets for focus groups, but we do have an audience in front of us.

Test out some of your core messages and ideas in social media posts. Share them in different forms - video, single images with a caption, a blog, all the different forms.

See what resonates and dig deeper into these.

Discard the ones that don't get traction.

Sometimes it takes testing to get these right.

You can also ask past clients, or your email list if they see truth in your core messages.

The key is to make these messages simple for you to remember, simple for others to understand, attractive to your target market, and in line with your offer and your position in the marketplace.

It all needs to fit together like a glove.

Here's an example of two messages for two different clothing lines:

"Affordable everyday essentials made for everybody"

And

"Luxurious, delicate merino staples, limited quantities available"

These are both for a very similar piece of clothing at first glance. One retails for fifty dollars, the other for five hundred. Can you tell which is which by the message? Which words would feel out of place if you switched them around?

Here's an example for an online group coaching course

"Perfect for time-poor, budget conscious startups"

"Premium group coaching, in small groups, with individual support"

Which one of these would you expect to pay more for? And why?

What could the phrase time-poor indicate in terms of the length and expectations? What would you expect to receive if an online course included "individual support"?

Here's an example for an electrician

"Affordable, friendly and reliable, available for maintenance and emergency call outs."

"Exceptional attention to detail, work completed to the highest standard, the finest electricians city wide."

One of these electricians is choosing to market to everyone in their area, the other to people who are prepared to pay more. Both can have a place in the same city. Which one would you choose?

Your words help paint a message and attract the right people. It needs to show how you are different. It needs to be brave. And it needs to be honest, rather than aspirational.

If your marketing is constantly attracting the wrong "perfect person" you've got a messaging problem. If it's attracting the right people but just not enough of them, you've got an amplification problem. For that, you need a WEB.

PART FOUR
THE TRUST BRIDGE

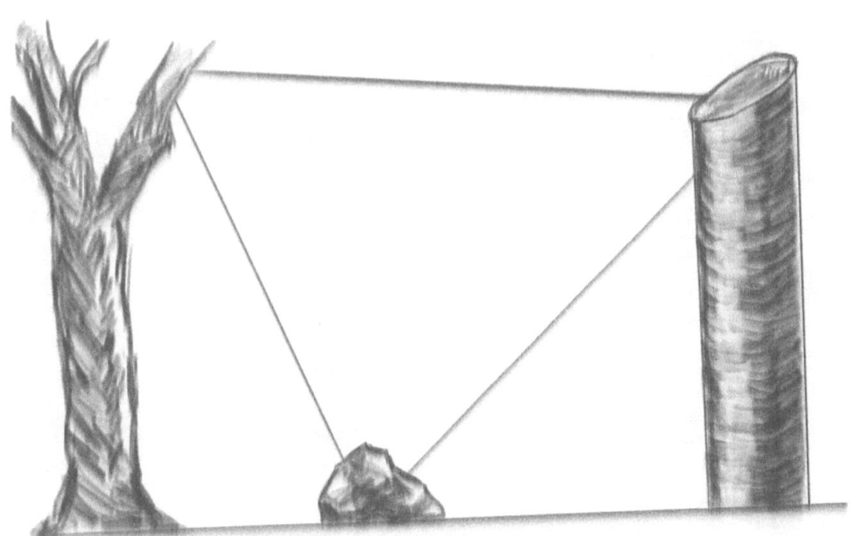

CHAPTER 14

THE TRUST BRIDGE

OUR WEB WON'T STAND THROUGH THE SEASONS, IN GOOD WEATHER OR BAD if it's not built well. It won't be a place where people feel safe enough to make decisions, unless it's built as a bridge connecting the two lines coming out from the anchor point of the message. This is our trust bridge. And everything we create relies on this trust bridge being strong.

A GREAT MARKETING STRATEGY STARTS WITH BUILDING TRUST

I'd like to say that the knowledge I'm sharing comes from a perfect business life, but it didn't.

Instead, it came from me making many mistakes, leading me to make a huge amount of changes in the way we do business.

There's so much talk about tricks and tactics, how to get yourself online, and what you need to be doing while you are there, but when it all comes down to it, the most honest to goodness important part of your marketing is finding out the best way to build trust.

Business owners are often embarrassed to tell me that the only marketing they are currently doing is word of mouth and referral business. For me, that's a sign the business has built trust in their customers and fans, and it's a sign of a healthy business. Turning on other forms of marketing will just increase the success.

Before jumping online and getting more customers, you need to check —are you getting people coming back? Or are you like the business owner I spoke to years ago who said "A new customer is one we haven't annoyed yet!" When people are telling other people about your business, it means they trust you will not damage their reputation with that person by doing work with them.

Before you go out to look for new customers, one of the simplest ways to grow your business is to remarket yourself to people you've already worked with. We once worked with a business owner who was struggling to grow, but had sixteen filing cabinets of files, each one a customer that they've never reconnected with! There was a gold mine in their business, right there.

If you've looking at your customer list and you're unsure they'd like to hear from you again, maybe it's because you're not sure you did the best job with them. That's a trust problem.

No amount of marketing will fix a business where you are bringing people in and then not delivering on your promises. Our job is to build the trust in our marketing, and then not break that trust when we do the work, or provide the products.

For us today, our robust client relationships are the bedrock of our business growth. They come back to do more work. They tell others that we're good to work with. This marketing is invaluable and key for a healthy business. And if it's happening in your business, I'd like to say well done!

WE ONCE FAILED THE TRUST TEST

Of course, as I've alluded to already, our business was not always like this. I used to go on Facebook and watch people suggesting anyone but us when someone asked for a marketing expert. Instead of thinking that something was going on, I used to think it was just because "our customers don't do that sort of thing".

It wasn't. It was simply because we weren't delivering on our promises. So there was no reason for clients to tell others to use us. We were a mediocre business.

I started Identify in 2015, and it grew super-fast without a huge amount of planning on my part. I went from working in the areas I knew really well, which included strategy and content writing, into running a team of fourteen, trying to manage workflows and wondering why everyone else was earning money except for me. As I've already mentioned, my pricing was out of whack, I was working in areas outside my skill set and I had poor boundaries. It was a recipe for disaster.

I was spending all my time trying to bring more work in to feed all the people I'd employed. Because I was so busy, I handed over the client relationships to my team, and stopped checking in to see if we were all delivering what we should have been. I created a machine that was all about just trying to stay afloat and it was no longer about the customer. I'd develop great rapport with a new client, and then they'd be handed over to my team, who were doing their very best to look after them, but with poor systems and checks and balances in place. In all, I was building trust in our marketing, but not growing it with our clients.

Our business was a mess. We kept on attracting what I was being told were problem clients. Which was weird, because I had thought they were awesome when I'd brought them in. The truth is they weren't the problem. We were the problem.

This is a difficult chapter to write.

First—it's not painting me in a great light! I have worked on my shame around this time, but there's still some there. And shame is the most unpleasant feeling. But secondly (and most importantly) it would be easy for me to lay the blame for all of this on my team. After all—they were the ones not delivering right?

Ahh, NO.

I strongly believe that a team is only as good as the leader. And this leader was a mess! I had never sat down and thought about what my values were and how these needed to underpin the rest of the business. Because of this, I was at the mercy of everyone else's values. Some of which did not align with mine. As we covered before, the values need to be clear to lay down a strong foundation.

I hate confrontation and avoid it at all costs. I also was (at that stage) a huge people pleaser and wanted everyone to be happy—which meant no one was!) Essentially, it was a big pile of messed up poo! It all came to a head when a key staff member left. I had to take over her role in managing clients and it was like the light went on. I very quickly wanted to turn it back off again.

We had only a few clients left. I'm really not sure how they stayed, though I'm so thankful that they did. But it wasn't enough. We had a team to pay, and we were now only billing seven thousand dollars for the month.

I did what any person would do at this point. I went to bed, popped the duvet over my head and hoped it would all go away. Of course, I was only putting off the inevitable. I had a big decision to make. Would I stay, and try to fix this? Or should I just shut it all up and go get a proper job. (At least I'd get paid!)

My husband Rod had left his job several months before and had a little time. He offered to lend a hand for a month, looked at the books and what we were doing. He sat me down and said "Rachel, this business is a mess. We have customers who work with us once and never come back. That's not how things should be." A light went on inside me and I could see what I'd been doing wrong. It was both the worst and best moment of my life.

I'd been so fixated on pulling people through the door to work with us, that I hadn't made sure they were welcomed, cared for and had their needs met when they arrived. I had been so busy trying to build trust to get new customers, that I had not noticed I had immediately broken that trust as soon as we started to work with them.

FIX WHAT IS BROKEN FIRST

Rod and I decided to try and undo some of the damage that had been done. While we got our little team working with the few clients that were miraculously hanging on, we approached the clients we'd worked with in the previous twelve months.

We started with an apology, acknowledging that we had not maintained a trust relationship with them through the whole process. We asked "What did you find about your experience with us? Did we deliver on the promises we made?" The answers weren't great.

Rod and I spent the next six months working with clients and re-doing the work we'd promised at no cost, and took time to repair the relationships we had broken. We could not afford to pay ourselves, but we knew this was us rebuilding a broken business.

We wanted to create a business that served our customers.

THE POWER OF RESTORATION

One of the clients we had reached out to was a woman called Tracey Smith. She had received work from one of our team members, and it hadn't delivered what had been promised. She spent time detailing several areas in which the project had missed the mark, and not delivered.

We listened and redid the work at our cost. Rod travelled to work with her face-to-face, to repair and then over deliver what we'd done. From this Tracey switched from being an unsatisfied customer to an avid supporter. She began to talk about us in Facebook groups and recommend us to other business owners.

Here was the power of maintaining trust in action. We had several people come to us, and work with us because Tracey convinced them to. We began to get referrals from someone who loved us!

This is the true power of trust. When you build it, maintain it and grow it in your business, your customers help get you more customers.

Tracey moved to Australia and continued to work in her business and other businesses, helping them in marketing and automation. We started to get new business in Australia from her continuous referrals and enthusiasm about us and what we had done for her.

Several years later, as we started to look for new strategists to join our growing team, Tracey was a natural fit. She knew us, she aligned with our values, and she knew the power and importance of building and maintaining trust. She now is one of our key marketing strategists, specialising in e-commerce.

Tracey moved from a place where we had broken her trust completely, to where we rebuilt that trust, and then to a place where we now have one of the deepest trust relationships possible in business, the one within your own team. The ability to honour the trust you build with customers is essential.

If you are in a place where you've got a graveyard of broken trust relationships in your business, you need to work on fixing that before you try to get more clients for your business. You can rebuild trust. It takes sheer effort. It is hard work. But it is incredibly worth it. Building trust builds great businesses.

TRUST ALWAYS STARTS WITH YOU

Trust. It's such an important part of marketing.

So much of this book is me talking about how important it is for people to trust you before they buy from you. To know you are the right person they want to lead them to a sale, that your brand does what it says it does, that their money and time is best invested in what you've got.

But for them to trust YOU, you've got to trust them first. The trust relationship starts with you.

To get them to trust you've got to give them the good stuff. You've got to share with them ideas, tips, maybe free materials. You've got to help them see what you have is good. You can't do that well if they can feel you holding the good stuff back.

Some of these people are damaged goods. They've been ripped off in the past by people who promised them something they did not deliver. You need to get them to trust you, and to do that you need to trust them, and the process, first.

You will be their quiet, gentle, and clear voice in their ear, trusting they will know how to act when the time is right.

And yes—To do this, you also will be giving your good stuff to people who are not your people. Some will try to steal your stuff. Some are not ready for you yet. And some are freeloaders who will never understand the value of paying you.

They could be competitors (you would be amazed how many other marketers download our free lead generation resources and come along to our free events—I take it as a compliment—as you should when your competitors do that to you).

Here's how I feel about it—if they take it and use it, it can't be the same way I do it. It will naturally attract a different person because they are different. And my job is to do it MY WAY the very best way I can. That's all.

The people who get your free stuff and hang around could be early to the journey. They might not be ready for you, but they aspire to be one day. They might browse your online store then go find the cheaper option elsewhere. Stick with them. They know you are the gold standard they are working towards. Trust them. And know that they are your biggest fans. They will live vicariously through every single person who chose you after their recommendation.

Or they might just be here for the free ride. They'll take everything you give away for free and gobble it up and ask for more. They help you define boundaries around what you give, and how you give. (This is one of the reasons I'm not a fan of the discovery call lead generation most coaches start with—there should be a filter, as it's not sustainable in the long run if you are building the trust journey correctly.)

Of course, the ones we really want are the ones who love us, choose us and are right for us. But for them to come, we need to trust each person who comes, we need to trust the process, and we need to trust ourselves and what we're selling. Until we've got that, asking people to trust us will be just an exhausting game of chase.

DON'T TREAT IT LIKE A ONE-NIGHT STAND

Long before I was a marketing strategist, I was a full-time writer. In this other life I wrote a book about internet dating. It was so long ago Tinder wasn't even around.

While I was collecting other people's stories for my book, I was also dating. A LOT. I learned quite a lot about the different feelings you'd get from the guys who were genuinely looking for something, and the others just tapping everything they could. One of the guys I met during this time showed me his records. Not the vinyl kind. The spreadsheet kind. He had made a very methodical spreadsheet of his conquests—how long he'd chatted to them, where they met, and the time it took for him to seal the deal. Many a business owner would be impressed with a parallel amount of dedication to recording results from their sales team. Although they'd prefer it was sealing actual business-related deals. Far less HR complications.

Besides the fact showing me the spreadsheet immediately prevented me from ever wanting to be a new line on it myself, it made me think about the difference between aiming for the one-night stand, or gunning for the long-term relationship.

One-night stands are easy. Turn on the charm, show your best side, target people who maybe feel a little uncared for... and you are in. Sometimes, if you're lucky you could cut all of that and just ask directly. For the right target market that may be enough.

But relationships are riskier. You've got to allow for the fact they're going to see your imperfections. You're going to need to follow up those phone calls, answer their texts, and show interest in things they are interested in. You've got to be consistent, even if it's just consistently average. You're going to have to be present, sometimes far more patient than you want to be, and somewhere along the way there's going to be some awkward conversations around commitment, and how it would look if something happens between you both.

And then you give it a go. Sometimes, it's the perfect match. Often, it's just great for a season—and you both leave the relationship happy about each other, just not needing each other anymore. And if someone asks "Hey, what did you think about that human?" you'll say something nice, even though they aren't right for you anymore.

Sometimes you both jump a little soon. You don't ask any questions, don't wait to see if they are really the best type for you. Every now and again it works out great. More often than not, it doesn't. No amount of sweet talking and love bombs replaces a reality that doesn't match up long term.

The pay off, of course, is having this incredible person who becomes someone in your corner, your biggest fan. And it's far less effort getting "repeat business" for a long period of time when they're secure that you are both invested. You'll even get more business after you've made a mistake (unless you make too many mistakes and then you may be out of luck!)

In the end, great relationships are built on trust, no matter what sort of relationship it is.

TRUST ISN'T THE SAME AS PERFECTION

When we talk about having trust-based relationships between you as the business owner and the customer we're not expecting perfection. I've made some doozy mistakes with clients who are still happy to be our clients. A trusted relationship is one that has room for disagreements, mistakes and mishaps.

I spent four years working with a client on her Facebook ads. Eventually she was confident enough to look after them independently. We were thrilled, as our focus is always on supporting a business owner to take charge of areas they are interested in.

About six months later, she came back and asked for some help with a particular campaign. This was one we'd built up together for several years. I logged in and started to talk to her through suggestions on a zoom call.

To this day neither of us are quite sure how it happened, but I managed to delete part of this effective, beautiful campaign that we'd both put hours of work into. To my surprise, the client laughed it off. She knew it was an unfortunate accident, and that I would be able to find a way to make it better. We had a robust enough relationship to trust through error. (As an aside, I promptly cleared the rest of the day and spent it rebuilding the deleted part, free of charge. That's part of trust as well.)

I've had disagreements with clients who choose a different path than I recommend. I sometimes have to give avoiders a strongly worded "ahem, how's it going?" message. Trust gives me the ability to serve our clients with everything we have, and helps them know we're doing it all because we care about them, and their business.

Trust builds better business relationships.

BE WARY OF CUTTING THE TRUST BRIDGE SILK

I'm the biggest procrastinator when it comes to doing admin. I'd go so far as to say that admin and I are not friends. But there is a special place in hell I reckon for "life admin".

I don't know how normal people do it. Remember to book the warrant of fitness, pick up the prescription, book a hair appointment, pay the bill, AND do the rest of our lives? What is this madness? I'm the kind of person who has, at this present time, seven pieces of incredible art my daughter's created in the boot of my car. I put them in there seventeen months ago, because the one time I went to get them framed, the shop was closed. It now feels too hard to get back there again. (I've also got a bag of clothes for the charity bins. I'm not sure what decade that popped in there.)

I started to gain some semblance of control over my life admin a few years ago when I discovered the power of advance booking. In November of every year, I get out my diary. I make a list of those regular appointments and important actions and I book them into my diary. I've used this method to book my hair appointments, monthly massage, and facials (priorities here), and even regular date night restaurant bookings and a monthly lunch out with my mum, for up to fourteen months in advance.

I know there are boring life admin tasks I've missed off this, but I've got a secret weapon—my husband. He realised pretty early on that if he booked a reminder about my Car Rego into HIS diary, it was more likely to get done.

The system was perfect for me (besides the whole "suddenly I'm in lockdown and everything is cancelled"). I'd spend ONE day working out my ideal schedule, and emailing all my "suppliers" for them to do the booking admin on their side. I'd then pop the confirmed bookings into my calendar and I was away! I'd then plan all my other stuff, such as work, completely around these jobs/"moments of luxury that still cause me admin pain" and it was magical.

Until my hairdresser left. Finding a hairdresser that's right for you is a very complicated procedure. When I find one that I trust, love and can relax with, I can get a little attached. I've had a few bad break ups over the years, when they've moved cities or countries. I followed one around five different salons over a three-year period, until I decided she wasn't the one. I tried the long-distance thing for a while when one of mine moved to a city three hours drive away. It didn't work out long term.

Eventually I found a place I liked. I found a hairdresser who just listened, then took over and sorted my hair for me. I could sit there, and know she knew exactly what she was meant to do.

Then things changed. The salon called me to say she was sick, and could we please reschedule the appointment. I said "sure". I'm not a monster. I know that despite her superhero skills at cutting and colouring she could get sick.

They then cancelled ALL OF MY APPOINTMENTS FOR THE YEAR without talking to me and sent me a text message to tell me my new stylist was someone else. If they had picked up the phone, filled me in and maintained a relationship with me I would have stayed.

I never went back. The trust bridge had been snipped, unlike my hair.

PART FIVE
THE DECISION HUB

CHAPTER 15

THE HUB IS WHERE THE DECISIONS ARE MADE

IN THE CENTRE OF YOUR WEB IS YOU. YOU HANG OUT IN THE HUB. THE only scurrying you do on your web is to build it, or change it. While you are there you might stop for a while and chat to someone hanging out on your web. In a nice way. Remember, you're a kind spider. You want your people to come to you, rather than chase them and wrap them in your spidey silk.

Soon we're going to build out your web, and spin the capture spiral. But for now, we need to make sure that our Hubs are the stickiest they can be. We want them to be uniquely ours, and help people buy from us.

While most of this book is about digital marketing, your Hub can also be a physical store, or office. It may even be an event, or an expo. Before we look at your online Hub (your website), let's look at your other Hubs.

WHY MARKET OURSELVES AT ALL? WHAT ARE WE TRYING TO DO?

Everything we do, whether it's old school marketing, digital, or using the power of other's referrals is all geared up to get people to make contact, take action and then buy.

With the growth of social media, some small businesses run their business completely from a Facebook, Instagram or LinkedIn page.

There is a huge risk to this as it's a platform that you do not own. You might be able to do business on it today, but tomorrow the platform may change the rules, delete your page, and break everything you created.

It's important that we use our marketing to move people to a place where they can make a decision without the noise of everyone else around.

WE HAVE MULTIPLE HUBS

It used to be you had a store or an office and that was enough. That and a big advertisement in the Yellow Pages. Now we have to spin our capture spiral and it's far more complicated.

We have multiple Hubs. Not just offline, but online too. We used to just have those physical places to create as our Hub, and then, once the internet arrived, we added a virtual office/store with our website.

Now we have mini Hubs everywhere and it can be hard to keep track. It's kind of like we've created a mega content web where each radius line leads all the way down to a door taking you into a segment of the Hub—one for Facebook messages, another for Instagram, LinkedIn, TikTok, the list goes on.

People can make a purchase without needing to leave their social media sites and it's tricky to get boundaries around where you're open and ready for business and when you want to step away.

It's a good idea to think through a process for managing all the different doors that people can walk through and how you'll move them to an email, a Z oom meeting or similar. It might not matter when the content web starts to attract more customers, but when it's fully built and catching people in great numbers, you'll need a system! It might involve using a scheduling platform that brings all your messages together, and using some automation, having an automatic message suggesting they email, or deciding you're on call 24/7.

All of those platforms can be powerful and effective for your business. In this book, we focus on your website because that is a platform you own. It's a place where you've got the control. You won't have your account deleted, or disabled overnight, unless you forget to pay your bills. You can choose what methods people can use to get in touch with you.

If we think of all those doors leading into your Hub, the ones from the website are definitely huge French doors, designed to be flung open to let in the hordes.

There are also a few Hubs we don't cover in this book, that you might also need to consider:

1. Your bricks and mortar store

Traditional retail businesses have operated successfully for years without needing a website. One of the benefits of using this as your core decision moment space (DMS) is that anyone who comes in can have a conversation with a real person, touch and feel the merchandise.

However, there are a few drawbacks of having this as the only DMS.

Just like online, you'll attract people at all stages of their buying journey from "I am not sure why I came here", right up to "I'm getting a frypan today, and I already know which one!"

If you are busy with another client, the potential customer is left to browse alone with no specific call to actions. If you stay busy, even that eager customer may leave the pan on the counter and walk back out.

You can't reconnect with them without them coming back into the store (unless you want to totally creep them out and follow them down the street with the frypan!)

And… if you're in a pandemic, you can't even let them in the door to buy.

2. Your physical offices

I'm always surprised when we get walk-ins at Identify. I'm not sure why—we have signage! But we're not really geared for on the spot appointments.

Your office can also be a DMS, but you'll tend to only attract people who are either right at the beginning of their journey (information collectors who can take a lot of one-on-one time with no return) or people already ready to go, missing out a large chunk of people who fit somewhere in between.

3. Markets and expos

Markets and expos can work in a similar way to a physical store, but it's hard to keep the relationship going if you aren't going back every week. If you can't show up, or they stop coming, you've lost a customer. As some of our clients found out, this type of DMS is also at risk of pandemics, and circumstances outside your control. In the end it's a space you do not own, just as a social media platform is.

4. Conferences and events

Speaking in front of a crowd is one of the fastest ways to grow (or break) trust with potential customers. If you've got an offer to sell, this is a great opportunity to pitch it, and sell it as an option to people who've bonded with you during the day.

If you hit the mark, you're likely to collect a few clients. However, there will be many more who may not be ready to buy from you today, and you might need to give them a little more than an Instagram account to connect with, post events.

I often consider conferences and events to be part of your capture spiral, along with webinars and online events. I then spin a radius line of nurture emails to help attendees reach the DMS.

All of these different Hubs are valid parts of your sales and marketing plan. All of them can see success, growth and create profit for your business. However, all of them will be helped with a website.

YOUR WEBSITE IS THE KEY HUB

Long ago, in the early days of the internet I worked as an internet marketer for some of the very first websites. This was when Google was only a toddler. THAT LONG AGO.

These websites took the long form letters some of you (if you're old enough) would have received as junk mail in your letterboxes as a kid. These sales letters were long essays, often punctuated with a pile of yellow highlighted text and dramatic call to actions in red, all geared to sell you their product and any amount as long as it ended in a seven ($197, $397, $1497…)

I helped write some of these websites. They were big on persuasive writing, had hardly any images and were relying on someone taking the time to read the whole thing from beginning to end. They helped shape my writing, although I was never a huge fan of the style. There are modern equivalents of these. A landing page for a course or a coaching programme uses the similar sections, though thankfully without the yellow highlight.

I also helped write for the websites that auto played cheesy music at full blast when you landed on the page, websites that used flash on slow internet and took an age to load, website that only looked great on a specific type of screen, websites that had vomited every little thing about the business on its 175 pages of glory and then of course, the "brochure site".

A lot of business owners still refer to their website as a brochure, a simple marketing electronic flyer to advertise their little part of the universe. For me, a website is a living, breathing representation of who you serve, why you are the best person to serve them and how you'll do it. It's the linchpin of your online marketing because it's the place people who've heard about you, interacted with you, and may already trust you a little come to make a decision. Will they connect with you today, take the time to come a little closer, or realise you are really not their cup of tea at all? This is where that magic happens.

It doesn't need hundreds of pages, fancy design, or clever technology. But it does need to make it easy for people to trust you, connect with you and take the relationship a little deeper when they are ready.

CHAPTER 16
NOT EVERYONE WILL CHOOSE YOU, OR WANT YOU RIGHT AWAY

IF ONE HUNDRED PEOPLE CAME TO YOUR WEBSITE TODAY WHO HAD NEVER been before, how many of them would take action and either buy from you, or phone/email you to start that process?

Statistically it will be between one and three percent. Some highly functioning eCommerce sites can get up to five percent. If it's a lot higher than that is normally because you are doing a lot of content marketing and trust building before they visit your website for the first time. Or it might be you aren't doing enough marketing. Often our clients reporting a high conversion rate have a small, engaged audience who are coming back and again, skewing the results a little.

If you want to get more sales without having to drive thousands of people to your website every day, you've got to think about the people who aren't quite ready to commit to buying from you yet. We're going to cover some of that in this chapter and later on when we talk about lead generation, but first let's talk about the people who won't choose you no matter what.

I don't like you.

Well—not YOU.

But that guy. Next to you...

Hmm... ok not him

But that woman behind you? Yeah, I don't like HER...

I like a lot of people.

Except for the ones I don't

Sometimes I really want to like someone. Everyone else likes them. But not me.

I don't resonate with someone.

It doesn't make that person wrong, of less value, not good at what they do.

They just aren't someone for me.

(Even if they are someone for you)

When I slip into trying to be liked by everyone, I remember I don't like everyone. And that's how it's meant to be. Because we are all beautifully different and some voices will resonate with us more than others.

Sometimes the most popular voice in the room won't be one that you resonate with. Sometimes you'll be more interested in that person in a completely different room. OR—That popular person is whom you connect with most. Both are ok!

(I do like you. HONEST.)

Just as your website will help the right people choose you, it will also repel between fifteen to thirty percent of your audience. This can be for all sorts of reasons. It's best not to get too obsessive about it. People are weird. And sometimes it's for the smallest of reasons! (I was once given a four out of ten score at an event from someone because she "didn't like my shoes". People can make decisions on the tiniest things.)

We want to work with people who need us, are ready for us, and align with our values. Your website needs to talk to the people who need you as clearly as possible, about the way you can best help them, and show them as simply and clearly how you can help them, so the right people choose you, and the wrong people bounce off and discard you as an option.

CATCHING THE UNDECIDED

If between one to three percent will choose you today, and between fifteen to thirty percent aren't interested, how do we target everyone else?

It's a big deal to email you, book a time, make the call or pop out the credit card to purchase. So we need to add in a few extra options for those who like you, but not keen to get that serious just yet.

Many business owners have an option to sign up for a newsletter or join up for a discount. This is a great idea if you are going to email them. (If you don't, you're mini ghosting a possible future customer!) You can also have something they can download for the price of their email address. Once you've got their email you can send them a series of emails to help them trust you more.

No matter what you offer, the key is to help each web visitor make the best decision for themselves as fast and simply as they can. Either stay and commit, investigate getting to know you better, or go find a better option.

SHOUTING LOUDER DOESN'T MAKE IT EASIER FOR PEOPLE TO UNDERSTAND

I don't know what possessed me, but a few weeks after the birth of my second daughter our little family packed our bags, left our little country home, and moved to Taiwan so my (then) husband could work as an English teacher and writer, and I could continue writing from an apartment on the twelfth floor of a large high rise in Taiwan.

Moving countries, changing cultures with a two-year-old and a newborn is tricky enough. Doing so without being able to say more than hello in your new language was beyond problematic.

We had to carry around a card with our address on it in case we got lost. We spent a night walking up and down a road that was meant to have restaurants on it and came home hungry because we couldn't work out where they were.

I would sit with the other mothers from the apartment block, and absorb the sound of them talking to each other, but didn't understand a word. I once saw a European stranger in a video store and ran up to him talking at a full rate of knots to discover he was German and couldn't speak English.

To be able to communicate with the people around me, I needed to learn the language. For a while I battled with my stubbornness. So I went for a "simpler" option. I turned into one of those horrible people who just tried to get people to understand by speaking IN ENGLISH louder, and slower. I learned something then that is very relevant to writing great website copy, and content marketing overall.

It is not about me. If I want to connect with the people I want around me, and help them understand who I could be to them, I need to talk to them in their language, not mine. And to do that I need to drop my desire to show off all my success, and tell them how great I am, and instead I need to show them how I can serve them.

It's all about telling your ego to STICK IT.

The old way of marketing was to tell people how great you are, so they could choose the best person in the room. This method underestimates our potential client's ability to choose the best person for them, rather than the official "best person."

We are not here to serve ourselves. We are here to serve the people who would choose us, refer to us, connect with us. And when we do that, and do it consistently, then the sales come.

One of the most powerful things to do when writing your website copy is to lay aside your ego, and instead show how you can serve. This feels counterintuitive because HOW WILL THEY KNOW YOU ARE ALL THAT AND A BAG OF CHIPS IF YOU DO NOT TELL THEM???

If we want people to trust us, we need to trust them first. We need to give them a story they can see themselves in, and see how we're here, ready to help make that story come true. We then need to trust them. Trust they will identify themselves in the story. Trust they will respond to it. Trust they will come to it in their own time, via their own pathway.

It's easier to write copy that just tells them who you are.

But it won't build trust with the right people in quite the same way.

CHAPTER 17

HOW TO WRITE DECISION-HELPING WEBSITE COPY

WE'VE GOT THIS SHOT TO HELP YOUR WEB VISITORS MAKE A DECISION AT the Hub.

Remember the other Hubs? The retail stores, the office, the expos? How do we invest our money and time to make these perfect to capture our ideal people? Imagine if we invested the same amount of energy and thought into our online store or office. Our website is an essential and important sales generator and deserves our time, effort and care.

Your website doesn't have to be a blockbuster, special effects masterpiece. But it does need to tell a story.

There are whole books dedicated to writing great website copy. And here I am, giving you a few paragraphs. That's also what I want you to create for your website. Short, clear and direct to the heart of the visitor content. It will help them know without a doubt that they've either come to the right place on the internet or never want to come back here again.

I like words. I can get a little wordy. My website used to be smothered with my wordy love. We used to have a website that was over sixty-five pages, not counting the blog! And visitors loved it. We were like a beautifully decorated department store.

The problem was, we were too distracting. Visitors would get stuck in the web I'd created, then forget why they came. Instead of a good sticky web, it overstimulated them and confused them. There were just too many things to look at. The average time people spent on our site was over eight minutes. It was a feat of information greatness.

We also got no leads, emails and sales from it. That was a problem.

One weekend I took that beautifully designed, fully packed website and I hacked it into little pieces. I didn't use my web designer (I can be a little impatient at times), and I reshaped the website copy and layout to do these things:

1. Talk directly to my ideal customer
2. Give them plenty of ways to take action
3. Remove all unnecessary distractions so they could either come further into our web, or leave.

Did it look beautiful? No, it did not. Did it work better? Why yes it did.

My sixty-five-page website became a website that showed a menu option of a home page, an about us page, a contact page, and a blog section. That was all. We've since added a few more, but you won't find a menu that has a whole heap of dropdown options to try and sift through.

Our website is there for one purpose only. To help our ideal clients come closer to the Hub.

The result? Within twenty-four hours, that hacked up website started getting enquiries. From our ideal clients.

(I later asked our web designer to make it look prettier! It's safe, for now.)

WHAT'S THIS GOT TO DO WITH COPY?

If you want to write great copy, you've got to be brave. Brave enough to throw out words.

And brave to make the website about your customer, and not yourself.

If you've done the work creating your anchor, you know your ideal client and what they need.

You know why they need what you've got. And all you've got to do is tell them that.

Instead of trying to write clever catchlines, start with simple.

1. Share a promise of what's possible

This could be "Teeth so white you'll want to smile all the time"

Or "Never have to worry about tax payments again"

Or "Clothes that make you feel great".

All of these have an outcome that the ideal client needs.

So give it to them as soon as they land on the website.

2. Show them how you can help them create that

We want your web visitors to trust you. To do that, we want them to understand what they can expect. For our website it's a simple "we meet with you, we make a plan, we implement it" which can work for many service type businesses.

It could be "We'll learn about your business structures, we'll set up your accounts, we'll help you stay accountable on payments"

or "We'll send you the teeth whitening kit, you'll apply it for two weeks, you'll get a smile up to thirteen times brighter".

3. Explain what they can expect from working with you, with a blend of features and benefits

Show them what end result they'll get from working with you.

4. Give them a little glimpse of what could happen if they didn't work with you

While I don't believe in fear-based marketing, I do believe it's a good idea to remind someone of the pain they're already in, and an alternate universe where they never get released from it. Here they are in a kind spider's web. What would happen if they got trapped in a nasty spider's web? Or just never did anything at all?

5. Show them why you're a trustworthy option

You can do this through testimonials, logos of your clients, logos from professional organisations, or awards.

6. And make sure you give them more than one opportunity to get to you at the Hub

We used to have a contact form at the end of our homepage. What a lousy place to put a DMS! It's now at the top, and then there are another nine or so other opportunities for people to come closer to the Hub as they move down the page. Our home page of the website is made with the stickiest silk possible. And yours should be too.

Here's a few more tips:

1. Avoid long paragraphs. Checklists, breakdowns and short sentences help people scan and know they're in the right place, without having to work too hard. We want to make this easy for them.
2. We now often have people reference the wording in the website during sales meetings. This is a surefire way to know that the sticky silk is working to draw them in.
3. We care about conversions over beauty. I don't care how gorgeous your website is, if it's not getting sales. I've seen some very ugly websites get incredible results. I don't wish such ugliness on you, but focus on the message before you focus on the design.

4. If you're not getting the right leads, and you know the rest of
   your spider's web is drawing people in, then the message
   needs to change.

A note for those who will outsource the writing:

Writing for the web is a skill all on its own. I've lost track of how many people come to us for a marketing strategy after they've spent a huge amount on a copywriter, only to discover everything they wrote doesn't talk to their ideal client, and is too distracting.

Your copywriter needs to be asking the right questions. Ask them to show you previous work. If all their other website copy is wordy paragraphs, they won't be the right fit for you. And give them permission to be brave.

BEWARE THE CAUTIONARY TALE

I mentioned before that it's good to give your web visitors a glimpse of life without you. The key word is glimpse. We're not wanting to turn this into a full production miniseries.

Old school marketing often talks about "pain points". I use the term myself. Pain Points are us identifying what our customers need to have resolved, what the impact of those not sorting out that pain is, identify what pains they have (from being too busy, having mother guilt, not having time to work out)

Working out what would happen if someone did NOT use you is an essential step in your marketing process. We need to know the cost of what happens if they do not choose you. And most importantly, YOU need to be super clear on this too. This is your secret weapon in marketing with confidence, it's the reason you are going to liberate them from where they are now, it's the hope you're going to give them, or the excited reaction when that parcel arrives.

When you ask yourself the question "What will a person miss out on if they don't buy from me/ work with me", you can start to check whether your product or service is something that's enough for them to give you money for it.

There's nothing wrong about telling people about the cost of not working with you too.

The issue with pain points is marketers sometimes like to really remind us of our pain to lead us to buy what they've got. It brings up an image of finding the other person's bruises, and pressing our thumb down into it, until the person squeals, and then saying we can fix that for them. I don't know about you, but when my sister did that to me as a kid, I certainly wasn't keen to go and play with her straight after. In fact, if I had, it would be creating a pretty dysfunctional relationship between us over time.

People might come work with us if we push them in their pain enough that they feel they must get it fixed up now. Sometimes we need to be reminded of our pain if it's an emergency. But emergency solutions make great stories, not great relationships. (Let me tell YOU one day about the night I almost died in an emergency room.)

So if you are talking to people's fears all the time, and they are already stressed, you'll not build a business where people want to come back again and again or tell everyone else about. And, if they do, you'll just be building a business of people who are in a high state of anxiety all the time.

High alert humans question your actions more, struggle to trust, query invoices, and often struggle to pay on time. If the humans you sell to are people who need a solution to make them feel better, the biggest gift you can give them is to make them feel better, make them feel they've got everything sorted, and you're their cheerleader.

You can point out the bruise. Just don't dig your knuckles right in there.

While it's so important to help identify what problems you are trying to solve so you know how to speak to them, it's not a great idea to then make all those problems the focus of your message.

It's the easiest thing to do of course. You could say "Don't be responsible for killing people with your car, get your brakes checked today" and it would make a memorable impact (the phrase, not the car!) You could also say it this way: "Keep you and your loved ones safe on the roads. Get those brakes checked".

One of these uses the pain point in a negative way. It tries to trigger an anxious response. The other tugs at the values of love, care and life. It's the same message, from a more positive stance.

We want to make sure the visitors on your web are aware of the pain of not choosing you. We do this without creating an abusive relationship. We are kind spiders after all.

CHAPTER 18
HERE'S YOUR MOMENT

Out of all the pages on our website, the About Us page is the most visited.

It's also the page I look for most on other people's websites.

If a website doesn't have an about us page, showing your face and explaining a little bit about you, I'll bounce off and go to another person's site. Even if you have what I'm looking for.

An advertisement for the most beautiful pair of pyjamas has been on my feed recently. I fell in love immediately, and knew they were destined to be part of my life. Excited, I clicked onto the website to find out who had created these treasures so I could give them all my money.

There was no About Us page. No story of why someone had created these sets, no photo of the designer. I could not trust them enough to buy.

I'm even more resistant to approaching a services-based business with no About Us page.

I want to know who is behind the brand. And I'm not the only one. Maybe you feel the same way too.

Us marketers love to use the phrase "People buy from people" and it's completely true. If we walked into your office or store, and no one was there, we'd walk out too. We need to see who you are, and get a sense of your personality, values and mission.

Take your time to write your "about us". Talk about yourself in the first person (I) unless you've got a team. Share your values. Tell a little of your story. Show your personality. If you've got a team, show their faces, and a little bit of their personality too. You could even add a video, or a series of images.

Just add one. You're the spider. You are the whole reason we've got this web! Who do we know who to contact at the Hub if we can't see you and get to know you a little?

THE ROYAL WE

If you're a solopreneur, it's tempting to use the word "we" on your website to try and look bigger than you are.

Don't. It's smoke and mirrors, it's weird and you should honour your web visitor with the truth.

CHAPTER 19

CREATE AN FAQ PAGE

WHEN I WAS FIRST TRAINED IN HOW TO SELL, WE COVERED DEALING WITH objections. I was taught this great analogy, that feels a little poignant, as I haven't been overseas since the pandemic began. It is still a great way to teach why we need to remove barriers to make it easy for people to buy from you.

Imagine you have gone on a huge overseas trip (sob), and ended up needing a bunch of extra baggage to bring back all your goodies. You have just arrived back home and are waiting to collect all your bags. You know you've got eleven of those suitcases waiting to come around for you, but you just grab the first three, and then head off home.

Wait! No, you wait for all of those bags, and then you can play the game of trying to balance them all the way back to the car, ready to get back to your cat, and beloved houseplants.

If you think of that traveller as your future customer, and those bags as objections, or barriers to sale, they need to get eliminated before they buy from you, you can see that it's really important that they collect all the information they need.

If you only help them with one or two, someone else (a competitor) might go take the other bags off for them instead, and get the sale.

What's worse is you made the job easier for them, by warming up the customer without closing!

If you are cold calling, or have large items to sell, you might need to have several face-to-face meetings to help get all those objection "bags" onto the trolley so they're ready to go.

If you're wanting to sell more to more people, one-to-one selling is a very expensive method, both in terms of time and energy.

This is where marketing comes in.

When we use our marketing to remove objections, and help make the process from "I'm aware of you" to "I need you and what you sell" simpler, marketing works smoothly. It can feel like customers appear from nowhere, and if you are in a service-based business, it can feel like a sales call is really just a formality. The better the marketing, the easier the process is.

One of the simplest ways to help remove those bags from the carousel is to add a FAQ page to your website. FAQ is an acronym for Frequently Asked Questions. And it's a powerful tool in your "customer converting" plans.

I'm embarrassed to admit that after telling hundreds of clients to have one, I only added one to our website last year. It's what I call a "stroke of the pen" task, a one-off task that takes energy to do, but once done it's there, and doesn't need much updating.

Every FAQ page will be different, as it's your amalgamation of the questions people ask, and the information you need to cover to help people get a clever picture of working with you.

Here's some things you can include on your list:

- Pricing or budget indicators for service-based businesses
- What you cover
- What you don't do (especially if you get asked a lot)
- Steps to working with you
- Delivery or returns process

- How people can pay for your services/ products

It's a good idea to frame the question as if someone was searching for it in Google (it's good for SEO too then).

When making my list, I read through my sales meeting notes to see what people asked for over and over again. I also thought about the enquiries we get through our website and social media. Lastly, I popped a post in our Facebook group to ask if anyone had questions they'd like to know.

While it's a "set and forget" action, adding to the FAQ page when you discover other common objections, barriers and questions is a good idea.

The power of a FAQ page doesn't stop here, however.

My FAQ page has fourteen questions answered on it. These are all questions that help us respond to common queries, filter out potential customers who aren't the best fit for us, and helps us display our values.

If I take these, and add a little introduction, and a short, simple call to action I've got content for a social media post. Add in an image for each, and I've now got fourteen posts I can post on all my different social media platforms!

Because this is core information, and it's evergreen (not time sensitive), I can then schedule one to go out weekly, and then just cycle through them again and again. With fourteen posts, I've got one post a week on all my different platforms sorted for good.

Which answers two frequently asked questions our clients ask: "What should I be posting on social media?" and "Can I repeat social media posts?"

If you know you could be doing a better job warming people up to buy, perhaps taking time to write a FAQ page should go on your list of things to do.

CHAPTER 20
REACHING THE HUB DOOR

BY THE TIME PEOPLE REACH THE HUB DOOR, WE'VE DONE ALL THE HARD work and now people are ready to buy from us. Learning to close a sale is different to marketing, and needs new techniques. There's likely a whole book just in that!

If we've allowed people to take their time to come to our door, the last thing we want to do is pounce on them as soon as they knock. Take it from someone who has definitely come in a little too eager more than once. You can quickly unravel the beautiful web of trust that has brought them so close.

One of the key steps we need to take is to remove any hard to budge objections. Earlier in the book we talked about the suitcases our customer wants to offload from the baggage carousel.

When my girls were little, I stood at the door of the Decision Hub.

I used to live in a small town in Canterbury, New Zealand.

I was a single mother and had three young girls. Life was pretty tough.

I used to struggle with making ends meet and I really struggled to have anything there for me once I'd paid the bills.

Luckily there wasn't a lot of temptation around. There weren't that many shops where we lived and there certainly weren't that many shops that had great clothes that I loved.

Then one day I went into the town and discovered there was a new clothing store on High Street.

I had just lost quite a lot of weight and was wanting to feel myself again and reclaim a little bit of my own personal style. I decided this was an excellent opportunity to go try some clothes on and see if I could find what I might look like if I stopped wearing my baggy shirts and track pants (and a magic wand suddenly appeared and I could buy something.)

I tried on a black dress that fit me to a T and made me feel fantastic. However, it was also $230 which really wasn't what I could afford back then at all. The shop assistant could see that I was very keen on this dress but I was not totally over the line. She asked me what was holding me back and I explained that it was a bit too much money for me to be able to afford right now and I would struggle to make ends meet for a couple of weeks if I bought it.

At this point I was still managing to remember that this was just a window shopping trip, but I was very close to losing that control.

The shop assistant could obviously see that I was wavering. When she discovered I was holding back as it was a little out of my budget, she had another question for me. It was this: "What about if you just gave your children two-minute noodles and baked beans for two weeks," she asked.

For a moment I wavered. I weighed up my responsibilities as a parent, my desire to be fiscally responsible, and then, I looked at myself in the mirror, made eye contact with the shop assistant and said in a tone far more confident than I felt, "I'll take it!"

Let me tell you about that dress. I loved that dress so much. I wore it so often it got holes in it and I was so sad the day I had to finally say goodbye to it. Was it sensible for me to give my children junk food for two weeks so I can get that dress? Possibly not.

But I can tell you this. That shop assistant did a magical thing that day when she convinced me to buy that dress. She removed my objections, she found a way for me to get a solution, and she got herself a sale.

(As an aside, I held a lot of mother guilt for this behaviour for years. My children all first heard this story at one of my events as teens, and all were quite put out that I hadn't done this more often. Not so I could have more dresses, but because they really used to love two-minute noodles for dinner and they were considered junk food in our home!)

When someone comes knocking on the Decision Hub door, they will often have objections to overcome. Sometimes they don't even know they are there!

Looking at your website and making it as welcoming and sticky as possible can help you reduce many of those. For service-based businesses, you may need to have a one-to-one meeting to help remove the last few pesky barriers to their decision.

One of the best ways to support your interactions in the Decision Hub is through showing a deeper level of your investment in anyone knocking on that door. It's time to show them just how loving and kind you are as the creator of your web.

CHAPTER 21

SHOWING THEM THE LOVE

SOMETIMES THE HUB BECOMES A LITTLE LIKE A TRAMPOLINE. PEOPLE JUMP down to the Hub, and look like they're there to stay, but they are really just going to bounce back up to the web.

Others will come visit the Hub, and then once they've worked with you, or bought from you, you want them to stay on the web so they can work with you again.

For people to stay, they need to feel you care about more than their money. They want to feel you're invested.

We want to build a long-term relationship with anyone who comes to the Decision Hub. Sometimes people turn up when they are not quite ready. We want to help them stay close. Some people come, work with you, and then want to hang around. They become your repeat business and your fans.

INVESTING IS YOUR LOVE LETTER

It's not enough to consider your web to be for first time clients. Your content web needs to also look after and nourish those who you've already worked with before.

We do this mainly through social media posts, groups such as Facebook groups, and emails. For us, making sure our strategy clients feel cared for has led us to create a portal for them, along with giving them free or highly discounted access to our regular online training.

It's far easier to grow a business that has a growing number of past clients in it, than to spend all your energy catching new people on your web.

One of my favourite parts about social media is that it is so social. A newbie can be encouraged by the conversations and comments with the regulars. It's kind of like you've got a bar, and the regulars are sitting there at the bar chatting to you, and that dynamic is appealing to the new visitors. They want in! Plus, they want to know why your regulars keep on coming back. (I've got to be honest, I'm fully visualising the bar from Cheers right now. And Norm. I know I've just aged myself immensely with that sentence. In my very tenuous defence, I watched it as a kid!)

Along with social media, your email list is a perfect place to nurture your past customers.

I once worked with a business who needed more sales. I asked them if they had an email list. They did not. They sold consumable products so email was perfect for them.

I asked if they had a customer list. They pointed to sixteen filing cabinets stuffed full of client files. They were sitting on a complete goldmine. They didn't need new clients. They just needed to talk to their past clients again!

My first job for them was to digitise those files and get in touch with the clients to check they were happy to be contacted via email. Just doing that netted them tens of thousands of dollars in sales.

The key to email marketing is to remember that, just as in social media, you are talking to one person. Make it personable and make it friendly. Please also try to make it short.

There is a huge difference between a newsletter and nurturing email marketing. A newsletter is all about you, even if you pretend it's all about them. A nurture sequence of emails is all about the needs of the person receiving it. It will make them feel closer to you. It will prevent them from moving away from your web.

THEY'LL EITHER LOVE YOU OR LEAVE YOU

When someone asks me how often they should email their list, I say "as much as you want to."

When someone says "that sounds like too much" I ask them if they have emails from some companies every day. I know I do. I've got a few companies that send me more than one email a day.

I don't open all of them, but I see them. They fit into two groups. The first are several clothing brands I really love. Some weeks I'll open them all, other weeks I won't. I also follow a few other business owners and marketers because I love the way they think. I've bought their book or course or signed up for a freebie. Again, I don't open all of them, but I open enough to be reminded they are there.

They don't annoy me. I like them. I like that they want to stay in contact.

There are others who only email me when they want something. I unsubscribed from so many email lists during the lockdowns in the early days of the pandemic, because anyone who'd even had my email address suddenly wanted to talk to me. I didn't want to talk back, so I unsubscribed.

If someone really loves your brand, they'll never mind you emailing them. If they are moderately ok with your brand they may unsubscribe, stick around on your social media radius lines then pop back onto your emails from time to time with registrations to events, or more purchases.

And if they don't like you, they'll leave you. And that's ok because who wants to love someone who doesn't love you back. Right? We've got boundaries on our sticky web!

NOT EVERYONE FALLS IN LOVE AT FIRST SIGHT

We need the nurture emails for people who've bounced onto our Hub, and aren't quite ready to stay and work with us, or buy from us. We want to look after them via email if we can because it's more intimate and personable.

We also want to look after them that way because the first payment they'll often make to us is their email address. And once they pay it to us, we can own that little snippet of an address. It is more protected than a follow on social media. There are numerous stories of huge accounts disappearing overnight. All the engagement, the followers, the likes, the comments gone. If that's the only place you build your community, you have built it on an unstable ground.

An email allows you to step a little closer, and take the time to show you're worth that payment. There, right in their inbox.

To collect these emails you need something to give them for their email address. It needs to be worthy of the price. You could, of course, give them something lightweight and generic, but this is your first love letter. You want to make it count.

A great lead generation resource is something that both your ideal client wants, but also helps them work out if they need more. I call it a "hole finder" . It's got enough for the people who don't really need you to feel good about it, but not enough to solve every problem for everyone.

My personal favourite format is a checklist. However, it can be a worksheet, a resource, a series of videos, a challenge. Anything that you want to create and deliver consistently for the payment of an email address.

Once they've given you their email address, you can send them a series of emails that add value to them, and give them support. These emails can also promote your products and services.

While some people use this as a reason to send daily emails for years, I prefer to send a series of five to seven emails over the period of 14-28 days with a specific goal in mind. Then these people are added to our master list and get a weekly email from us.

Every business has different needs, and offers so what works for me might not work for you.

A lead generation resource works for all types of businesses. We've seen it work with coaches, strategists, retailers (style guides, recipe books and how to's), and engineers. The frequency and types of emails after the gift is delivered are all different but the basic format is the same.

I've created a flowchart and added it to the **beaspiderbuildaweb.com** website for you to download and use as a guide.

DON'T BE A TRAPDOOR SPIDER

I love myself a bargain. I'm the one who will always start with the sales section. There is something so good at getting a bargain of something you covet.

I once famously bought a very expensive dinner set when I was an impoverished student. I was THRILLED I'd saved $1050. Never mind I'd spent $450 at a time when I could least afford it!

(As a side note, I loved it so much I never wanted to actually use it. It travelled with me from home to home until I discarded it after my tastes changed. Apparently hand painted, easily chipped, non-dishwasher safe stuff isn't as "timeless" as I'd convinced my nineteen-year-old self!)

I love my bargains. But I'm incredibly suspicious of free. Free is never free. Free costs someone something in the long run. If it's not me it's costing, it's you. A free gift on the internet is rarely free. Neither is a free event. It will cost you your email, your time, your effort.

There is no doubt that free gifts work to build a list. But I don't want to build a list of free-stuff seekers. I want to build trust. Because the email is not the payment. The true payment is trust.

If I give you my email for a download, I'm trusting it was worth it. Will it be? Or is it just a ploy to get my email? And will it leave me wanting? Will I feel gravely disappointed? If I do, that trust is going to ebb.

And if the emails start to come hard and fast and they are all sell sell sell I'm going to know it's a trap I must avoid at all costs! Because I've become a victim of the trapdoor spider[1], and all I'm going to want to do is escape/unsubscribe and avoid where you hang out from now on.

There is nothing worse than finding something that is offered for free, and then, once you've got it, discovering it was a trap designed to slowly suck out all your hope in the kindness of strangers, vaccinating you against ever trusting the word FREE ever again.

Yet this is exactly how so many of our "free" downloads work.

The moment I create something for free, I know it's got to do three things:

1. Be valuable for every single person who uses it
2. Filter out the people who can work this stuff out on their own/ are just researching/ won't use me
3. Build trust in us, and know it means they'll get more goodness if they come work with us.

Your free download or gift or event has to help earn you the right to sell to the person who got it/ attended.

And they'll let you know when that is.

All you've got to do is keep on giving them the good stuff. Feed them up with trust building actions, just leaving a little bit back for them to keep them there another day.

KEEP IT PERSONAL

No matter how big or small my team and business gets, our nurture emails are signed off by me. Even if someone else wrote them. (I'm still writing most of mine, but someday I know they'll be outsourced to someone who actually proofreads them. Most of my emails come with a disclaimer about the typos you're going to find in them.)

When I'm writing an email, I do two things. First, I switch off my "this is what they need to buy" thinking and focus on what value I can give the person I'm sending the email to. And second, I focus on writing to just one person.

Here's a secret—I have done exactly the same thing through all of this book. I've imagined you with this book, and I'm writing it just for you. Sure, other people will pick it up and read it, but right now it's just me, writing down my thoughts for you to read and then apply.

We want people to feel valued, appreciated and looked after because we do value and appreciate them, and if they work with us, we will look after them. That's how it all works.

So don't say "hi team", use first names occasionally if you've got them but not obsessively in every single sentence, and when you're writing your emails write them to one person. If you can't picture who that is, choose a favourite client and write as if you're talking to them.

We send a sequence of emails after our MAP IT action plan training. It's a full day online, and I get to know most of the people pretty well, even if we've got a big crowd. We do a live walkthrough of what the nurture sequence they are going to get looks like. I tell them that every time we run the day, even though everyone has seen it's a sequence of emails I've already written, someone will forget I didn't write it personally to them, and email me to apologise for not reading the last one, or tell me I was magic for knowing exactly what to say to them today.

We talk to one person, even if hundreds of people are getting the same email at the same time.

And it's ok if they don't open every one of those emails. I know that there's enough in there to suit everyone, and not everything will be a perfect fit.

EMAIL IS AN ENTRY TO A SECRET PORTAL

I've lost count of how many clients say "yes" when I ask if they do email marketing, and then tell me what they really mean is they send a monthly email out to a list.

To me, that's completely missing the point of making most of the gift you've been given when someone provides you with their email. They weren't asking you to blast them with your news every month, with piles of links to your website and a generic message.

They're wanting something more, even if they don't know it, and wouldn't be able to explain it.

They want you to create an email marketing web, that is your secret hidden world, underneath the public content web you've spun.

Just like the public content spiral, you will continue to build trust, develop relationships and have people at different stages of the journey. You might have the "general population", the clients, the past clients, the VIPs and each segment will need something different from you.

Some will prefer a relaxed frequency, and others will prefer to hear from you all the time.

The book has been written to focus on the sticky web you're building out here, most of it in the public eye. But don't underestimate the secret world of email. Some of our ecommerce clients get thirty percent of their revenue from email marketing. Our service-based clients can get similar if they have a repeat business model.

PART SIX
THE RADIUS LINES

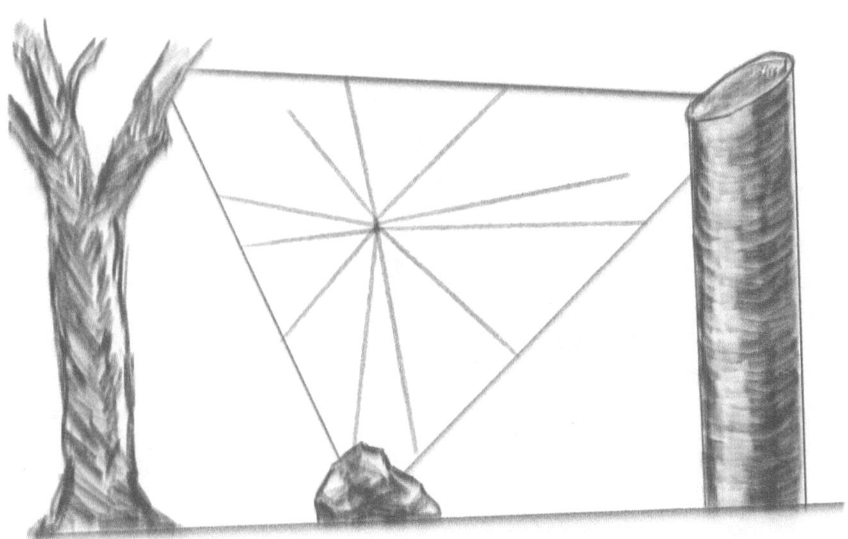

CHAPTER 22
SPIN THE RADIUS LINES

From the Hub we're going to build our web of content. The radius lines are all the types of marketing you're going to do to capture people and move them towards the Hub. These could be social media platforms, a podcast, a networking group or email. In our marketing strategy and action plans, we incorporate both on and offline marketing activity.

While I don't label myself as a digital marketing strategist, I know that most of our marketing activity is going to be on social media or with digital marketing. These are easy entry platforms (although some of my clients would dispute that social media is easy), they are low cost, (again, sometimes disputed!), and they give you great reporting. Being able to see what's going on helps you easily to track the return on investment. They also help you connect directly with your customers.

For those of us who don't serve a specific geographical area, social media also helps us be found by the right people for us. For those of us who are weird, quirky, or just completely unique, this has made it easier for us to find our people. It's made our world small.

Our radius lines are the platforms we use. Mine will be different from yours. They completely depend on where we find our best customers. Some business content webs are super simple with only a few lines connecting the Hub with the Trust Bridge, and others will be a complicated structure. Both are just as good as each other, as long as they are leading the right people to the Hub.

HOW I'VE BUILT MY WEB

I was going to show you a picture of my web for this book. I then realised it might stress you out as it has many radius lines. I'd call it a pretty complex web these days. But it once was very simple, and yours should be too.

When I was training as a teacher, we had to study a lot of educational theory. Some of it is now outdated, some of it made me furious, and other parts stuck like glue.

One of the frameworks for learning came from Jerome Bruner, an educational psychologist who coined the term "scaffolding" in the 1960s. Essentially it means that we start by teaching a basic concept or practice, then as the person becomes fluent and confident in that space, you can add complexity, layer on layer until you're able to create a really complex solution from that simple beginning.

I loved his philosophy and not only applied it to my teaching and parenting, but also to my own life. When I'm frustrated at learning a new task, I sit back, and try to break down the skills so that I can start at a simpler level.

Here's how we do this with our clients.

If a business owner has LinkedIn as part of their web, we'll break down the tasks over time:

1. *Optimise their personal profile (using our guide)*
2. *Connect with others (using our guide)*
3. *Start a habit of hanging out on LinkedIn and reading other people's posts*
4. *Start to comment in depth on other people's posts*
5. *Set a goal to post once a week*
6. *Grow the frequency of posts and diversify the types of posts created.*

And so on.

The speed in which a business owner may get this into place depends on their confidence with the platform, their speed in prioritising this as a new habit, their confidence in sharing their own thoughts and perspective, and their confidence in content creation. One might be up and using the platform like a pro within three weeks, and another will still be building up to regular posting six months later. Both can still see success from the platform as they develop their skills.

Everything feels hard when we are learning. Nothing feels comfortable because it's all new and our brain hasn't worked out how to take shortcuts in its thinking to help us to know how we move our bodies, access the files we've stored inside our head, and learn the process by heart.

I'm now able to produce an immense amount of content very easily. In fact, I create more content on a weekly basis than I'm able to put everywhere. It feels as simple to me as breathing.

It wasn't always that way.

WE ALL START AS MEDIOCRE BEGINNERS

At school I struggled to get work done. I found writing a drawn out and painful task, and deadlines were something I'd spend more time dreaming up excuses about than trying to meet.

I loved class discussions. They were my preferred way to learn. That, and art. But ask me to write more than a sentence at a time and I'd struggle.

That little girl would never have believed the older version of herself would write thousands of words a week. She'd also never believe she'd be able to perform with confidence, love public speaking without that rise of panic in her chest, or work out how to edit her own videos.

Understanding scaffolding as a young adult helped me see that to get to excellence, you've got to pass through a whole heap of beginner's mediocrity first. I'm constantly pushing myself to do more. The moment I become fluent in a type of content creation, I either dig deeper into it to find a new skill I need to add, or I move to a new form of content.

My web will look very different to yours because I've been weaving them for years.

The first one was very basic, with a monthly blog, some posts on social media that may or may not have related to the blog, and the beginnings of an email list. Now it includes podcasts, and columns, blogs, video, lives, posts, nurture sequences and more.

And I'm still not satisfied. Three weeks ago I had a meltdown when I realised I'd completely abandoned an important piece of my content web, and spent a furious Saturday afternoon sorting it out, all the while making a list of skills I still need to develop to do it better.

I will never be satisfied, because I crave to innovate, to find new ways to weave a web that's sticky for just the right kind of person, and I want that person to feel like each post, each video, every single email is written just for them, even though thousands of others have also seen exactly the same information.

My web is very different to yours. It's probably more complex than it has to be too! A very basic web can still be big enough, strong enough and sticky enough to catch all the ideal people, and draw them to the decision-making space, right there at the Hub.

THE BARE BASIC WEB

If you're new to web weaving, and making things sticky, you need to start slow. Jumping into weaving an advanced design isn't a lasting solution. Content marketing is us layering the new on what we already have, pushing against the pain of new skills and learning while resting on the scaffold of consistency, habit and confidence. We layer it up over time, and we start with the parts that will give us the best return first.

This is exactly what we do when we work with a strategy client. We prioritise which radius needs to be built first. We also prioritise where they need to build the strongest parts of their capture spiral (which is coming up soon). We check the framework can be built with strength and flexibility (narrowing the arrow), and that the business is operating smoothly.

If the business is an established business, we check the Hub is nice and sticky. Then we check email, because these people have already had a relationship with the business, and are already on the sticky part of the web.

Then we focus on one social media platform. Then another. Everyone wants to jump in and do everything at once. (Well, I do.) But when we build all the radius lines at once, all we get is a tangled mess of silk threads, instead of a well laid out web. You'll either give up or worse; redo it all.

I hate it when I have to repeat a task. I'm an editor's dream as a writer. I like to hand it over, let them snip away, and then just give them a huge round of applause for preventing me from living through the agony of repeating my work. Because of this, pacing myself and my team has become an essential skill of survival.

So when you build your web remember; We start with the bare basics, and slowly build up the web, layer on layer, radius by radius until it's a complex and intricate pattern no one wants to walk away from.

CHAPTER 23
IT'S TIME TO GET SOCIAL

I KNOW YOU PROBABLY WANT ME TO TELL YOU EXACTLY WHAT SOCIAL MEDIA platforms you should be using for your radius lines. I'm going to tell you right now, that I'm going to disappoint you.

For thirty-seven dollars I can buy a package on the internet that gives me a "everything you need to get your social media perfect" plan, posts and guidelines. I know, because I've bought some of them.

I'm often amazed at how much amazing content there is in one of these offers. I love getting them and pulling from them ideas (remember we're ARMED to help our web), and modifying them for my business. I know what to keep, and I know what to discard, because I know what's meant to be on my web, and I know what radius lines work best for me.

But I can't tell you what platforms you need to be on, because each one of us will have a different content marketing web, that's custom made for your clients.

What will suit you, will not suit the next person who reads this book. Plus, new platforms, and new ways of using platforms are changing all the time. The platforms I use and spend my time building a community on have changed through the years.

Last year I worked with a high-end jeweller who's strands of pearls sell for twenty-five thousand dollars. While she does have a presence on Instagram, because that's a natural fit for beautiful, visual products, we also recommended she learn how to use LinkedIn for business, as her target market tends to be professionals, who are employed, and are paid a very good salary.

Because there aren't many people making pearl strands using LinkedIn, she was able to add this to her web, and not be crowded out by other webs all trying to do the same thing.

Sometimes the best place to build a web is where there is the most traffic, and the most people to catch. And sometimes, it's best to be that SURPRISE web, you walk into when you least expect it, because WHY WOULD A SPIDER MAKE THEIR WEB THERE???"

In this book we've walked through how to work out what your message will be, and who needs to hear it. We've also talked about what to think about when building your web. But the next step—working out where to build it?

That's a you job.

I'm not leaving you completely alone! Here's a list of things I use to work out which platforms I'd recommend to our clients when we're writing them an action plan.

1. Where the bulk of your customers are likely to be

All of the main platforms share demographics around users and user behaviours. While demographics aren't everything (as you'll remember from our work on our ideal clients) they can help make generalisations around who you are likely to find.

You can also use Google Analytics, or surveys you'd conducted with your best customers to help work out where your ideal people hang out.

Do remember it's the people who are going to BUY who are our ideal web stayers. This is one of the mistakes people make when using other people's Facebook groups for a bulk of their marketing. It feels good, because you get a lot of feedback and responses. We like engagement. We need leads and sales.

2. Where the other spiders are

The easiest place to start to build out a radius line of your web is where all of your competitors are. It can be a quick way to work out how you are different, because you'll need to show why your web is better to hang out on.

For any small business, not being where your competitors are, can eradicate you from being considered. If most of your competitors are using a particular platform, then your future community knows it is a great place to hang out on those kinds of webs.

This is the concept behind shopping malls, where you can go from clothing store to clothing store without having to pop in your car to go to different destinations.

Even if your business is most definitely worthy of being a destination store, where it's hard to get a park, and you're not open all the time, but you are still the coolest store around, it's still a good idea to have another store in a place with high traffic too—because our radius lines need to attract people at every stage of the content spiral.

3. Your own preference in social media platforms

Earlier this year I worked with a coach, who works with creatives. Her ideal clients tend to hang out on Instagram. Most of them know they need it for their own businesses. So I strongly advised her to build up her community using Instagram.

Problem is, she (strongly) replied, that she HATES Instagram. I put it in her plan anyway, and told her (in a nice way) to suck it up, and be where her clients are. It made complete sense to be there and was the easiest way to build her web.

On paper, it looked like the best decision. She had a huge catchment area, and her specific message was perfect for them.

In reality, it sucked.

She hated it with a passion. She couldn't build up the joy she needed to do regular lives, although she really tried. She was sporadic in her posting. She was frustrated in having to use a platform she didn't love. Plus, because she was on Instagram, it meant that she'd likely also need to advise people on how to use Instagram for their own business.

Essentially, I had recommended she build a web that had made HER feel trapped, wrapped in her own spider silk, and she was having all the goodness sucked out of her. It wasn't a case of suck it up. It was a case of "escape or be consumed".

A few months back she canned the account completely. She's using a mix of blogging, and a bit of Facebook, and building up a community the way that fits her.

Is she building a web that is in the best place to catch her ideal clients? No. But she's still catching clients. It might be harder, and less of them are hanging out where she is, but she's in a happier place.

And happy spiders attract far better clients.

4. Your level of social media confidence

I've had a long-term love affair with digital marketing. I started with chat rooms, meeting people all over the world. I worked with some of the original internet marketers. I was blogging over twenty years ago. My first website is something I hope never sees the light of day, and was filled with highlighted yellow copy because that was how we did it back then.

My first Twitter account was when there were under a thousand users, and I hung around for a few weeks, then logged off. By the time I created my second account (because, typical for me—I completely forgot the logins for the first one) I was very much one of the millions, but I'm sticking to my story that I was a very early adopter when it came to Twitter!

I love learning, am not too stressed about looking like an idiot while I'm applying that learning and am pretty confident in how it all works.

I know that's not how everyone feels.

I watch the stress of my clients, terrified to press the wrong buttons.

I've seen people worry about what happens if someone comments on a post (and asks if they can just block everyone).

I've watched people struggle with the technology, the concepts, the tricks, the skills needed, the type of content, the set-up, absolutely everything.

And I understand it because I feel all of those things too when I'm learning.

But it's easier because I'm confident it's going to be ok.

We are all at different levels.

For me—I'm enjoying editing, thinking about special effects and how to tell better stories on video.

This past year I spent time with three separate clients helping them get used to seeing their face on a screen.

I had another who struggled with having to use her phone

And yet another who really struggled with content

We are all at different stages and places, and no matter what I say we all SHOULD be doing, we've got to start from where we are. If you're a true beginner, there's still time to learn and grow.

And if you've advanced and super confident—then keep on innovating, and pushing yourself.

5. Your commitment to learn, and develop

As I complete this book, I'm also setting some personal stretch goals for me in digital marketing. One of them is to really get a hang of YouTube. Over a holiday break a few years back I spent a few days setting up my channel right, and had full intentions to make it a focus and then that ol' pandemic came and upset all my plans!

So this is my year to learn it. I've been listening to podcasts, watching other creators, bought a course or two, and am planning.

I'm going to be pretty terrible at first. In fact, some of the videos on my channel are already at this stage!

But hopefully, in a year's time my videos are going to look more polished, and edited and good.

I'm a huge believer in learning how to use all the different platforms myself, because our emphasis is on being able to run your own marketing—and if I'm having to outsource it all to make it work, then I'm not going to confidently be able to teach it!

I don't know if it's my juggle of work and family, my workloads in general, my age, or the constant changing across everything digital, but I often find the rate of change and keeping up with everything is exhausting.

I read and spend time online every day to keep up with the play—but the truth is so much of what's out there doesn't need to be taken on board right away. Knowing what to let go is just as important as knowing what to pick up.

I used to drive myself into a massive bedrock of anxiousness until I worked out that it was better to focus on one or two types of marketing at a time and go deep than run around trying to keep up with everything.

Now I'll choose one platform or topic (like writing captions) and go deep on it. Then I move on, keeping a little eye out every now and again for any big changes that might upset all my learning.

The key is to make learning part of your routine.

Here's a few things you can do to make learning easier:

- Block out learning time in your calendar (prioritise it)
- Mix exercise with listening to podcasts, YouTube videos and audio books (this is my favourite method)
- Play the above options in the car on commutes
- Choose one to three people in the area you are learning about to listen to, and go deep with them

- Take everything you learn and measure it up to your strategy, and your goals. If it's not going to help make those goals a reality, then discard it.
- Focus on learning through doing, and playing. Use the A.R.M.E.D process in Chapter 26 to help you embed your learning.

PART SEVEN
THE CAPTURE SPIRAL

CHAPTER 24

THE CAPTURE SPIRAL'S CHIEF PURPOSE

THE CAPTURE SPIRAL'S JOB IS TO HELP ALL OF THE RADIUS LINES MOVE people closer to the Hub, every step a little stickier than the last. Depending on the radius lines you are working on, the capture spiral may have a concentration of activity in different parts of the spiral, from "not very sticky" to "suction-sounding stickiness". All of it is geared to do one thing. Get people to the Hub.

Last year I went through a huge stage of comparisonitis. I was struggling because I could see all these other social media accounts just build massive audiences while mine was only growing at about five percent a month. I fell into the trap of looking at their numbers and not my results. I interviewed and spoke with a few of the people behind those accounts to punish myself further and find out exactly how well their businesses were doing.

The first didn't even have a business. He was just building an audience for the fun of it. The second had an agency like mine, had been in business as long as me, but was losing money, and the third was "reinvesting" everything back into his business, and wasn't taking anything out.

I hope you can tell from what you've already read that I believe our job in building a web is to add value, add value, add value. And it is. But the purpose behind that as a business owner is to create leads and sales. Otherwise what the heck are we doing this all for?

We've got a C.R.M (It's a database with our clients) that we use to manage our sales pipeline. One of my favourite parts of it is the way it tracks where people come from. We know if they've come from Instagram, or a referral. We measure it all. It helps us see what marketing is working, what we should invest more time in and where our best clients come from.

The best thing about building a powerful content web, and being a patient kind spider is that by the time someone comes to the Hub, they are often completely ready to get started.

Your chief purpose is to remove objections and make spending money on your product or service the best decision imaginable. If you do it right as a service-based business, you don't need to have multiple sales meetings, spend time one-to-one proving your value, and you'll have a steady stream of leads in your sales pipeline.

The vast majority of our leads come to us this way. I've had to learn to ask people about how they found out about us, because if they just saw a Google ad, came to our website and then got in contact, they haven't experienced the beautiful comfort and relaxation of our web and have just jumped straight to the Hub. These people need some help to trust us more, and if I don't know this, I'm going to rush them and lose them.

CONTENT STATIONS ON EACH PART OF YOUR WEB

If someone was meeting you for the first time, would your conversations be different to the ones you'd have with your best friend? The way we talk to someone in our marketing changes depending on where they are in their relationship with us.

On a web, the further away they are from the Hub, the newer they are, and the more casual our relationship. When we're creating content, we need to think about what stage of the relationship we're talking to, and create content for each step.

The way we use each platform changes the way we talk to people too. For example, Instagram reels can be used both for people to notice you and connect with you. It's hard to use them to nurture your audience and outright sell. But you can use stories to nurture and sell, in conjunction with private messages. It's the same platform, but just different parts of it.

I learned the hard way to stop fighting how platforms wanted to be used. I love creating educational content. But someone who doesn't know who I am may not want to take the time to notice it if they haven't already had a few short, relaxed experiences with me first. This is why short form video has exploded in terms of use for small business owners. You can entertain and attract people to your account —and as long as you've got some other related content there for them, they will come and follow.

The four steps to the Hub looks like this:

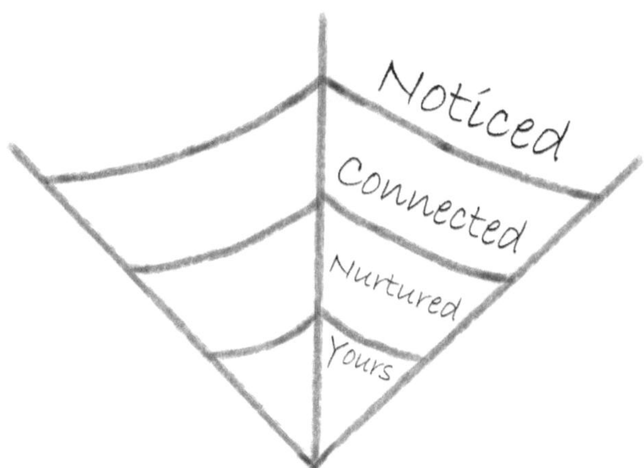

THERE ARE NO STRAIGHT LINES

We know human behaviour is not logical. So remember that most people will move back and forth along a radius line, jump off and go see your content on a completely different radius and then come back.

They may move closer, then away again over and over again before they make the decisions to come see you at the Hub.

CHAPTER 25

BUILD YOUR CAPTURE SPIRAL IN STAGES

THE CONTENT YOU CREATE FOR EACH PLATFORM NEEDS TO TALK TO different stages of the customer journey. Most platforms will need to have a mix of content to serve all stages, and others might only serve a few of them.

The breakdown of the types of content for each stage also differs depending on what your goals are, how best to use that platform, and what stage you are at in your business, or introducing your offer.

You can use every style of post for any stage.

THE FOUR MAIN STAGES

NOTICED

The content for this stage is light, designed to be attention grabbing, is often entertaining, or stands out as different. We focus on relatable content.

The end result is people notice you, follow you and connect with you on the radius line.

To encourage them to take these actions, we use call to actions such as:

Follow me, Like this comment, or Subscribe to my channel…

CONNECTED

The content to nurture people on our web is where we start to get sticky. We offer high quality insights, ideas, and information, designed to help remove obstacles. We want the content to expose gaps in their knowledge, and help people see a need for you and your expertise or products. The focus here is on educational content.

The end result is to help people stay connected to you, and start to engage with your content. This includes liking your content, and starting to comment on your posts.

To encourage them to take these actions, we use call to actions such as:

What do you think? Tell me, comment below, tag someone who, share with…

NURTURED

We are ready to get super sticky. The content is warm, and relational. It encourages people to give their own advice, or replies, and answer questions. The focus is to build trust through motivational, feel-good content.

The end result is for them to come closer to trusting you, or stick around after they've bought from you before (if you have enough of these people they can help all the newbies on your web make their way down the radius to the Hub.)

We get them to take action with calls to actions that require more thought to reply. These can include: What did you learn, check out, download, tell me…

YOURS

These people are knocking on the door of your Decision Hub and just need those last few objections taken care of. For these people we need to express our offer as clearly as possible. To do this we use promotional content.

The end result is they become a customer!

To get them to take that action we use call to actions such as: book a time, sign up for, use my code, buy now…

Below is a chart version of this. You can also download a version of this chart on **beaspiderbuildaweb.com.**

e.g.

	STAGE	PLATFORMS	CONTENT TYPES	THEIR BEHAVIOUR
NOTICED	Get them to visit your web	Highly engaged social media account/s	Short form video. memes. memorable images	Liking posts. following your account
CONNECTED	Help them feel connected on a Radius line	Social media platforms	Carousel posts. posts with captions. blogs. longer subtitled videos. stories. lives.	Commenting. watching stories. participating in lives
NURTURED	Take them across other lines as they draw closer	Other social media. Move to email. Visiting website.	Stories. lives. direct messaging. lead generation. blogs. free webinars/courses. groups.	Sign up for lead gen. attenting webinars.. moving to other platforms. Direct messages
YOURS	Arrive at the hub	Direct messaging Email CRM	Email Stories. courses. groups	Buy your product or Message or email you to talk about meeting

When I'm creating a content marketing strategy, I think about how to make the most of any time and energy I'm putting into content creation. I want people to love hanging out on my website. But I also need them to come talk to me at the Hub, and that means I've got to make sure I'm creating pathways to make that simple for them.

At each stage of the journey, we need to consider four key areas:

1. The frequency

How often I'm going to post content that helps that stage of person notice me, and be encouraged to follow me. Whatever I choose will need to be consistent, and all the messaging needs to stick within my "narrow arrow"

2. What platforms I'm going to use

I'm going to think about the best platforms for my target audience and work out which ones I'll use at different stages of the journey. I'm not going to list everywhere I'm posting my content, but look at my specific strategy for one or two platforms for each stage.

3. Content types

I'm going to identify what types of content I'm going to use at each stage. Some of these work across all platforms, but others work best at specific stages. For example, short form video works best on the outer parts of the content spiral, and longer, more educational video works better closer to the Hub.

4. Their behaviour

I need to know it's working. So I work out what behaviour I want them to have at each stage. For example, if I've created content for people to notice me, the action I want them to take is to like my post, and follow me. If they're at the Hub, I'm going to want them to be ready to buy.

When you know your core message and offer, you can use this to plan out your content types and key call to actions on your chosen platforms. I've included a graphic that shows how I'd use this for Instagram. (We've also got all of these as printables on **beaspiderbuildaweb.com** so you can download and use the template option.)

We use a similar framework for each line of business, e.g. coaching versus one-to-one strategy, and if we've got a special launch going on.

This also helps me remember to add a call to action at the end of posts, and which one is best for which type of content.

It's super important to create a plan that fits your capacity, your ability to stay consistent, and what outcomes you want to achieve. The worst thing you could do is simply copy mine and use it that way!

BUILD YOUR WEB
EG: INSTAGRAM

	FREQUENCY	TYPE OF CONTENT	CORE MESSAGE	CALL TO ACTION
NOTICED	5 reels/week 1x meme daily engagement	viral reels ujsing tending content. memes. commenting on big accounts. solid bio	Marketing models Marketing terms Confidence with video	SOFT: FolLow me Tell me Like if you agree..
CONNECTED	2x carousels 3xfeed posts per week	carousel posts showing insight. and single posts adding value.	Marketing models Marketing strategy insight Tips and hacks	Tell me Share with me Check out my stories
NURTURED	Live 1x /week Video 1x /week Stores 5x /week	instagram lives. instagram video. instagram stories	Indepth tips and ideas Requests for feedback. Podcast Column and freebies. FB Group	Replying to prompts in stories Download my.. Private messaging
YOURS	1-2x /week	direct messages. move to email. special offers. links in bio	Our products Our webinars Our online school and coaching	Book a time Buy my thing Sign up for...

Use the worksheets on **beaspiderbuildaweb.com** to plan out how each radius line fits into your sticky web. You might have gaps in some areas as you learn about your idea platforms. This is normal.

Once you've filled out one for each radius line, it's a good idea to keep them nearby. I like to have these to refer back to when I'm creating my content. It helps me remember to create content for each stage of the sticky web journey to the Decision Hub.

CHAPTER 26

THE STEPS TO CREATING THE CONTENT FOR YOUR CAPTURE SPIRAL

To make a sticky web, we need to create content. The most effective way to do this is to create a content bank. I felt I didn't need one for a long time, because I do find creating content easy, but since I created one, I'm feeling far happier about my marketing. I can have a really busy month, and fall behind on content creation and know I've got a bank of content waiting for me.

I also use this as a place to put my content ideas too, so that I don't have to be inspired, create and post all on the same day.

Here's the steps to keeping yourself on track with your content.

1. Name your niche/core reason for business

Remember to narrow the arrow. It might be marketing strategy, life coaching, civil engineering, bookstore, or any business focus.

2. Choose THREE key sub-niches

These need to reflect your anchor points, make sure they are building your trust bridge, and fit in with your "narrow the arrow" offer from Chapter Twelve.

For example, you might be a hairdresser and choose the following: looking after your colour, short cuts, and updos. A life coach's three might be: Identifying your values, the power of meditation, and how to know you are out of alignment.

3. Make four buckets for each sub-niche

Now take those three sub niches and choose four main topic areas you can talk about within those.

Here are examples of this from recent clients:

NICHE: Health and Fitness App

THREE SUB-NICHES: Mindset, Fitness, Nutrition

AN EXAMPLE OF FOUR TOPICS: Mindset: Managing stress, Habits, Meditation, My Own Journey

NICHE: Sales Trainer

THREE SUB-NICHES: Communication, Sales Tips, LinkedIn

AN EXAMPLE OF FOUR TOPICS: Communication: Self talk, Team Talk, Customer Talk, Prospect Talk

This can take a little getting used to. I've included a downloadable handout on **beaspiderbuildaweb.com** to help you work through your own content buckets.

MAKE TWELVE LISTS OF TEN

One of the simplest ways to create a huge bank of content is to use the "ten things" trick. If you can't think of ten things you know about a subject, it's likely that it's not going to be a core part of your business.

Get a piece of paper, or a doc and brainstorm ten things you can say about each topic. I had to do this a bucket at a time over a few weeks. Some of them were easier than others and some I had to use the A.R.M.E.D process I'm about to teach you to fill in.

If you find there are far more than ten, you might want to group them into smaller groups, so for the hairdresser, it might be looking after your hair after it's been lightened, regrowth, and bright semi permanents. (I'm going to admit I'm getting nervous choosing topics as a non-hairdresser. I'm purely going through what I'm curious about!)

These lists of ten become your content. You could write a blog or do a podcast or video about all ten. You could choose seven and turn it into a carousel post. You could choose three, or five or more and turn it into a short video. You could choose one and do a single image post, or short educational video.

You can use, reuse and reorganise that list over and over again, and create a huge amount of content with it. You could even turn it into a free lead generating document and collect emails.

You can take one list of ten and turn it into:

1. A carousel post/BLOG/ podcast/ video of ten points
2. Choose one and deep dive
3. Chose two and compare
4. Choose three and list
5. Choose five and go deep
6. Choose seven and create a high value list
7. Choose nine and create a downloadable lead generation download.

You can change the focus, change the stage of the journey you're focussing on, change the call to action, but use the same ten ideas over and over again.

IT'S TIME TO BECOME A.R.M.E.D

Before we dive into my A.R.M.E.D process, I do need to declare I come from a long line of pacifists and using this anagram is messing with my head a little, even though it's my own making! However, I use the word ARMED in a fully non-destructive way in this situation. (Thank you for allowing me to explain myself!)

To create original content is almost impossible. Even with new changes in technology all the time, there are thousands of people putting out the same material, often faster than any of us can attempt.

However the way we can stick out and be remembered is to create content that provides an original outlook, or describes an idea in a fresh way. This is what I'm doing when I use phrases such as "Be a Goat in a Tree", "Be a Spider, Build a Web", and "You Can't Kill a Man with Your Face". I'm helping people understand and remember concepts they may or may not have grasped before. I break down areas my clients have barriers to, and help them apply to their business. I also make it easy to attract people who understand the way I communicate.

We all have our own unique methods to explain ideas, or describe products. Our words help people paint a picture of expectation, and when we share our own thoughts, we naturally attract people who like how we think.

I follow a lot of people in my industry, but only if they are people who inspire me, enhance my creativity and help me learn. If they give me an uncomfortable feeling in the base of my stomach I don't go near them. I try not to follow local competitors. I want to make sure I'm not influenced by their content, and start to create content that is either similar, or feeds off theirs defensively.

I want to be inspired. I want to learn. I know that my best ideas will often come from someone else's idea, content or knowledge. I also know that my content will also do that for someone else.

Last year I bought some materials off an amazing marketer, Kate Toon[1]. She has created a range of frameworks for marketing. Before I bought the products, I emailed her because I knew buying the products was a risk.

Even if I'm using a product for my own use, it's inevitable it will influence my teaching, and work with my own clients. I know that I might one day write a blog, a chapter of a book, or create a resource that would have been affected by her products.

I didn't want her to one day see something I created and think "Damn you Rachel, you thieving cockwomble." So I let her make the call of whether she wanted me to buy her product, knowing I may create my own materials after being influenced by hers.

Thankfully she replied that while they were not to be "sold as your own templates or given away", that they were designed to be used. She accepts that they may influence new material. With that sorted, I bought them, have used them all the time, and have since adapted some of the materials, putting my own spin on them for our clients to use.

This is the essence of being A.R.M.E.D.

We are being influenced by other people's content all the time.

Here's how it works:

ABSORB

I'm a sponge when it comes to information. I spend time on social media platforms reading and learning. I take snapshots of great ideas, and take notes from them. I have a file where I add inspiration. I watch accounts of knowledgeable people. I have an Audible subscription and try to listen to a book a month. I listen to a podcast on my walk every morning. I'm absorbing, I'm learning, and I'm taking it all in.

To create, you need to have something to create from.

One of my friends Paul has worked as the head of marketing for some international companies. He told me a great story about a struggle the owner of one of these companies had when trying to get his creatives to innovate.

This owner gave his team the worst brief for any creative. "You have a blank piece of paper, and three weeks. I want to see what you do!"

Three weeks later the team presented their work to him. Or rather they gave back the blank pieces of paper. Paul explained to the owner that it's hard to create out of nothing, and a brief (like the frame threads on a spider's web) would help give the creative a starting point.

The owner picked up one of the pieces of paper, squiggled on it and put it back on the table and said "There! Here's your brief." Three weeks later they met again, and lo and beyond, the team had a range of incredible designs and ideas.

We need to have something in our head to make new things in our head.

NOTE:

I now have more time than I have had in years to research. Please be kind to yourself if that's not true for you. There are seasons to learn. When I was working, and a single mum of three young children, reading a book or getting enough time to listen to a podcast while awake would have been impossible. My books of choice back then were young adult dystopian fiction. Nothing makes you feel better about toilet training a two year old than reading about the near death of a sixteen year old who's magical powers make them the perfect candidate to save the world!

I've worked hard to carve out learning time as part of my work life. It's a cost to our business, and I'm aware it's not a luxury we all get to have. Do allow this book to be your absorber material however.

REFLECT

One of the biggest mistakes people starting out in content creation make after they absorb is to just copy the work. They might change a few colours, and perhaps a few words, but the work is essentially the same.

This is because they've missed an important step in the creative process. The time to reflect. When I listen to a podcast, I will pause and take notes. These are sometimes direct quotes, or ideas. If I then jump online and start to use these, and do not credit them to the source, I'm a thief.

Instead I pop the notes away, and then bring them out a few weeks later. My head is no longer filled with the voice and nuances of the iringal speaker. I take a look at what I've written (and hopefully it's not something like "asnOICNAEI DNVIEFNVA Dandd;ngrj" which can happen if I try to write as I walk.) Then I think about that idea in relation to my anchor points.

MODIFY

It's time now to modify that content and make it my own.

The sayings and phrases in this book are me modifying a message to tell a story my way.

Let's be honest, I could just say "Be more confident about showing your face on camera" but it's funnier and more memorable to say "You've never killed a man with your face."

Or "Be a Spider, Build a Web" is more interesting than "How to create a content strategy"

Modification of the message helps the message become yours. As it spreads people recognise it as yours.

I have followers who send me spider videos, stories about webs. They know it's my message.

When I was researching for this book I found out there's already a thing called "spider marketing". The idea of using a web for your content isn't necessarily unique.

But I also found MY way of describing the spider's web for your marketing was new.

We modify to make the message something we own

EXPRESS

Once we have our message, we are ready to express it, and we need to over and over again

To explain "Be a Spider, Build a Web" I've filmed short videos, long videos, told stories in presentations for webinars, created single posts, created infographics, and have even written a few songs! I've now gone full committed mode by writing a whole book about it.

Our expression of our thoughts through words and images is how we spin our threads from the radius of our web.

DISTRIBUTE

We don't want to use the information once, we want to maximise all our hard work.

We take the content and find all the ways we can use it on our capture spiral.

We might post a short form video to Instagram, TikTok and YouTube, Pinterest, Facebook and LinkedIn. One piece of content, across six different radius lines.

If it's a single image, we could post it to Instagram, Pinterest, Facebook, LinkedIn, use it in an email, and possibly as an image for a blog post of the same topic.

That blog post could go on the website, also be placed on LinkedIn and a blog site, be linked to in an email, and also linked to on Facebook, LinkedIn, and Pinterest.

We could then read the blog post and make it a longer video, and post that too.

The express and distribution parts are the more easily outsourced, and is how the content spiral becomes your powerful tool.

To make it really strong, we need to make sure we ARM ourselves first.

CHAPTER 27
WRITE A CAPTION PEOPLE WILL NOTICE

Our content is what makes our web sticky. The more memorable it is, the more engaging it is, the more people will stick around.

One of the hardest parts of being a business owner these days is the consistent need to provide content. The time, the effort and the process can feel painful, and uncomfortable to many. It was bad enough when you needed to get a monthly blog together! Now it's all about writing captivating captions for the images you've managed to cobble together.

In our Facebook community MAP IT Marketing, and with our clients, we know that one of the biggest blocks business owners have is that they need to write a good social media post (more than once, and taking much less than an hour for each one.)

I was originally worried about writing about this topic because these days, when it comes to writing, I'm a massive content overachiever. These days, writing is as comfortable to me as breathing. It's currently 10:15 a.m. and I'm writing this chapter. I've already written my weekly column, four to five social media posts, and a Facebook ad.

But it wasn't always that way. In school I used to struggle to put a pen to paper, and get my words out. My brain would swing from not being able to formulate a single sentence, to having so many thoughts in my head I couldn't decipher one from the other.

When computers became commonplace enough for me to be able to type out my words rather than write them on paper, my life changed. Even though I find my brain sorts out my thoughts better on paper, I find it hard to get my words out fast and legibly enough (ask my poor team who often have to decipher my scrawled notes!), so typing on a screen helped my output.

But really, what helped most was that I had to find a job that I could do from home after having children, and discovered my brain really liked the structure and freedom of freelance writing. (Plus the reward of payment at some point.)

We can find it hard to find the motivation to write a social media post because no one is giving us a deadline of "must be published today" and who knows if that post is going to actually work, be seen by the right people, and get you a sale.

It can feel pretty disheartening when you lavish your all too short amount of time on a post, to find three people see it, and no one commented on it. No one is there to cheer this SACRIFICE to serve them. It's heartbreaking.

HERE'S MY 'HONEST TO GOD CAPTION WRITING PROCESS'

(Ok, this is one of them. The other one, which I used today was to have a nap, dance around the office, eat a peach, take myself out for a coffee and spend two hours scrolling on TikTok. I'm figuring that's not one I should recommend you follow…)

I'm going to teach you a framework to use in your own writing, because it's one I know works and it's one I have used in the past.

I do use elements of it all the time, but I wanted to offer full disclosure as I know that you're likely to read this book, then go read a social media caption or two of mine and be filled with an incandescent rage of disbelief that my post was NOTHING LIKE

THIS PROCESS AND I AM TRYING TO TRICK YOU. And I'm not. I promise.

Years ago, I was a primary school teacher, and discovered that I was far better at teaching P.E. than art, even though (as you've heard) I'm a heffalump when it comes to exercise, and I do love to create. It's often easier to teach as you learn, than when you're an expert, because then you still remember the steps, and are all too conscious of the brain pain you are inflicting on the learner.

Last year I was challenged by a desperate client to work out how to teach her how to write a caption. So, after a few days, I came up with a five-step process, after studying many captions from marketers I admire.

But I'm a fluent writer. I start with a hazy idea that percolates inside my head. Sometimes it doesn't come out when I need it to, although having a distinct time that I'm allowed to release it does help it be ready. It doesn't have words, or even an image. I'm experiencing it right now as I write this paragraph and the best way to explain it is it's a hazy, shifting blob of an idea, moving around in my head. As I put my fingers on the keyboard, I feel words come out, almost on autopilot.

Sometimes they reorder themselves halfway through a sentence, sometimes they come out perfectly. Sometimes they write something I didn't even plan to write at all. I can write like that for hours. I'm now what I'd call a "fluent writer".

People who are fluent can mess with the structure, cut corners and often do an inferior job than a learner following a process. We're relying on our experience and our instinct. Sometimes it makes a near perfect post. Sometimes it's going to result in a complete miss.

I've been known to rewrite a heading, or add in a call to action well after I've posted because I've forgotten a crucial element.

The way I write isn't going to help you learn. When we are learning, it's much easier if we have a framework. So that's what I'm teaching you in this book.

I'm going to teach you a caption writing process to help with:

- Instagram, Facebook and LinkedIn captions
- Fleshing out a script for a short video for TikTok, Instagram, YouTube or anywhere
- Setting up the basis for a more in-depth piece such as a blog

It works with every type of business, and once you get the handle on it, can help you write captions faster, and with more intent.

I do recommend you set aside regular blocks of time to write. Most of us writers know we write in some places better than others. I wrote part of this book in a cafe, which is one of my favourite writing environments. Besides the conversations I desperately want to eavesdrop, I'm in the zone, and I know this is my writing time.

Though writing comes naturally I still often don't like it. I can struggle to start, and I will do almost anything else to avoid it. So adding structure helps. I've also found they are times of the day, or even times of the month I write better than others.

One of the most liberating things I did as a small business owner was realise I needed a regular diary time to write content. I also realised if I focussed on one bucket of content at a time it made it far easier.

I prefer writing on paper when I'm learning, so if you are like that too, use our downloadable caption writing worksheet on **beaspiderbuildaweb.com**.

I'm going to step you through the process below, and then give you some examples of the headlines, and the call to actions to help you create your own scroll-stopping post.

STEP ONE: THE HEADLINE

Besides the image for your post, the headline is the best way to get people to slow their scrolling and start reading.

It needs to talk to your target audience, tell them something they'll find interesting and leave them wanting more.

Using superlatives (or as I like to say "show-offy descriptive words") or declaring the number points you are going to cover.

5 clever tips to help you write an incredible caption

Change the number, change what type of tips, change the content

e.g.

3 favourite ways to wear your high-top sneakers

7 quick meals you can make with halloumi

Time is tight right now? Here's one thing you can do today to improve your captions

Change the "base need", the number, and the solution you are promising

e.g.

Got all the sweatpants you need right now? Here's three reasons to get a pair of these ones

Money is super tight right now? Here's what we did to make things easier

Ever wondered what it was like to work with a marketing coach?

Change the type of service or change to owning a product

e.g.

Ever wondered what it's like to engage a financial advisor?

Ever wondered how you could write your own course?

Ever wondered what it feels like to own your own custom painting?

Ever wondered why people rave so much about slow cookers?

I'm completely obsessed with Canva at the moment and this is why

Change the "feeling" and the subject

e.g.

I'm completely over sending quotes at the moment and this is why

I'm totally excited about this new opportunity for our existing clients and this is why

I'm so addicted to buying Dutch liquorice at the moment and this is why

Today is the day I'm going to let you in on just how I get all my captions for the month written in an hour

Change what secret you'll share with them

e.g.

Today is the day I get to share with you our brand-new range of planners

Today is the day I get to tell you all about our new staff member

Today is the day I get to show you just how well these new pants fit a curvier body

STEP TWO: THE HOOK

The hook takes the topic from the headline, and explains what you're going to experience in the rest of the post if they keep on reading.

STEP THREE: THE JUICY CONTENT

This is the body of the caption, and is where you need to give value, information and insight. I am a list lover, so my information tends to be in bullet points for easy scanning, but you can write this in paragraphs too if you prefer.

STEP FOUR: LINK TO WHAT'S NEXT

We're about to ask your reader to take some sort of action. We want them to keep reading at this point, so this section helps connect the information you've shared already with a request to act on it.

STEP FIVE: THE CALL TO ACTION

Every post needs a call to action. It can be direct (such as buy now) or it can be softer (give me your tip or advice).

It's a good idea to create a range of calls to actions, as we don't want to sell on every single post. People are more likely to comment on a post when they don't feel sold to all the time.

Let's put this all into action

Below are two examples of social media captions that have been written with this structure.

Here's a completed example for a product-based business:

"My Favourite thing about Winter is definitely merino cardigans

It's official! It's getting colder now so it's the perfect time to layer up

Here is why I love cardigans:

1. Instant layers
2. Can easily squish into a bag
3. Can add a pop of colour on a dreary day
4. Can wear buttoned up or open (so versatile!)

That's why I'm so excited about the cardigans that have just landed in-store!

Check them out—just click on the image above to shop!"

Here's a completed example for a service-based business:

"The most defining moment of my life was learning this truth:

No matter what you do, not everyone will like you. So you may as well just be yourself.

Here's how to show up as yourself more:

1. Take time to define who you really are. (You might have forgotten it after trying to please people for so long.)
2. Unfollow/ignore people who don't get you, and aren't nice to you
3. Connect online with people you respond to, and admire
4. Comment on their posts and get to know them
5. Enjoy positive feedback when it comes
6. Invest in an empowering photoshoot for your business brand.

Sometimes it takes a little extra help from someone like me.

Know you need this?

Send me a message and we'll set up a time to talk."

I suggest starting with the options I've supplied in this book, to write your first caption or two.

Once you've got the hang of it, you can try to play with the structure a little more and make it uniquely yours.

NO BUSINESS IS TOO BORING.

One of the craziest parts about our businesses is we always completely undervalue just how curious people are about what we do. You might think you have the most boring business in the world, but you could be the only one!

In fact, if someone tells me their business is boring, I'm immediately interested to find out why. I want details!

It's not that you have a boring business, but boring content comes from you thinking it's boring, or being bored yourself. If we create content with a negative mindset around its value, it's not going to attract people to it.

I always think it's like being a goat in a tree.

These goats live in Morocco and love the taste of Argan berries. When the berries ripen, they eat the ones they can reach and then the goats climb up into the trees, and chew on these fruit. They swallow the nuts inside whole and these are passed through and fall to the ground, where farmers can then harvest them for the argan oil inside.

Tourists loved the goats so much that now farmers will sometimes lift the goats into the trees to attract photographers.

Now I didn't know any of that when I started being fascinated about these goats. I just loved looking at photos of goats in trees. Some might say I became obsessed!

If we ignore those poor goats being used to fuel my need for more images, and focus on the greedy hungry ones instead, we can just imagine what would be going on in those goats' heads.

They're not thinking "oh I must think of something interesting to do today for the 'Gram'."

No, they are just doing what they do when they are hungry. They are doing their job. And it's generating business while they do it.

I'm here wanting to see all the photos. I have questions. I want answers. I'd love to ask a Goat what it feels like up there, what they can see, how they balance. I'm curious.

We are all goats in a tree.

We completely take for granted our boring business because we're in it every day. But our ideal audience? Well they've got questions. And that makes our content anything but boring.

CHAPTER 28

IT'S GOOD TO REPURPOSE CONTENT

If you've written a caption with this process, you'll end up with a piece of content that's simple enough to repurpose into a short video, or a visual post.

I'm going to take that one step further. Let's go back to your twelve lists of ten.

We're going to create a meaty piece of sticky content. This could be a blog post, a webinar, a YouTube video, or a podcast. I've used this process for all of these and more.

This year I'm focusing on YouTube. This is partly to help me develop skills on a platform I've previously avoided, and also to create content faster. As I record my video, I use a tool to transcribe my recording as it's made. I can then use this to help write more content, and get direct quotes for social media posts. I also use it to create subtitles for my video recording, and I load these up onto YouTube, when I load the video up.

I often write a blog on the same topic, and get my team to load it up to one of our websites. We will probably add the YouTube video at the bottom of that blog for good measure. I get my team to repost the blog to my LinkedIn profile, with a link back to my website. While I'm writing the column and blog, I highlight quotes that pull out some of the key ideas in the content.

With this content sorted I can get my team to:

- Turn the quotes into graphics
- Cut the audio and video of the podcast into clips
- Create short form animated and basic audio tracks
- Use the material for inspiration for fresh short form videos
- Take an idea from the content and turn it into an infographic
- Take a series of information for a series of images (a carousel)
- Find images and write captions on the topic

I then schedule and share this information out on every platform I'm currently working on. Some of them use nearly all the forms of content, others one or two. I put the same content on more than one platform as much as I can.

This is a web I'm making that I have been building for months. I started off with creating a big piece of content. I then slowly built habits and activity around adding new ways to repurpose it.

If you are just starting out, a good goal would be to:

1. Write a blog
2. Pull out three key points and turn them into social media posts
3. Use these same three key points to create short videos (Reels/TikTok/YouTube videos)
4. Pull out two sentences you like and turn them into quotes for a graphic for social media.

That gives you nine pieces of content from that one blog already. Of course, you can do far more, but this gives you the beginnings of a stick, content marketing web for your business.

You can download an infographic showing the ways you can reuse the same content at **beaspiderbuildaweb.com**.

REPURPOSING HELPS ME SERVE MY AUDIENCE

If we're building a web, we need to think of our core messages just like the spider silk. No matter what shape you weave, and where you make it, the content base is the same. It's just going to look a little different every time the web is created.

How you like to learn and relax on social media may be different to the next person. The way we're consuming content is constantly evolving.

The irony of me writing a book about marketing is that I now normally listen to an audio version. before reading the print copy. It's my hope that once this book is all published and more than my family have bought a copy, that I'll be able to do an audio version. I love reading, but I also enjoy listening. I listen to podcasts every morning on my walks. I can watch TikToks for hours, enjoy great storytelling, and beautiful images on Instagram.

I struggle to watch long videos, even though I make them and some of my followers love watching them. I don't enjoy being part of most webinars, even though I love to run them.

We all have particular ways we learn.

The single biggest mistake business owners make when looking at marketing activity is only making content the way they like to consume it.

We're not serving our target audience by only doing things we like. We're not marketing to ourselves! We already have ourselves around. We're looking for new people. Who will one day pay us?

To find them, we've got to create content they want.

With written, video, static image design and audio formats so accessible to us it's become so important for us to create content using different formats, and post on different platforms. That's a big job, but using one meaty piece of content to create from makes that job a lot easier, and delivers a more consistent message.

BATCHING MAKES IT ALL POSSIBLE

I definitely prefer to create my content in batches so that I maximise my time. I'm easily distracted and some days I'm either not in the mood, or booked back to back. I'm also working on moving towards a business that doesn't need me working in it every day, so I need to think ahead a little.

I used to batch my content in weekly or monthly sections, but I found that made it hard to juggle all the different forms of content. When I went through the same "narrow the arrow" process you did, then created my twelve content buckets, I realised that most of my content is very much "evergreen".

Evergreen content is content that can work today, next week and maybe even next year. Some of the chapter headings in this book came from a post I wrote first on LinkedIn, added to my content bank and then shared on other platforms multiple times.

All businesses can use evergreen content. For some of us, nearly everything we create can be evergreen. For digital marketing, some content is going to date. For a high fashion brand, you might only get away with twenty-five percent of repeatable and timeless content. For all of us, having a bank of it ready and waiting is the act of a truly clever spider.

This is the process I batch my content.

1. I start with one of my lists of ten
2. I check my content calendar and select a type of post, form of content, like a single image, or a video
3. I check in with my content ideas list, that I made using the A.R.M.E.D method
4. I check in with my ratio of Noticed, Connected, Nurtured and Yours
5. I write out a plan for each post.

Then I batch my steps of content creation. This means I can create faster, and I'm not shifting from one type of post to another. The other benefit of this is that one form of content will also then help me create a different form super easily.

First, I choose one type of marketing content such as short form video, or carousel posts, or longer form video and plan out the content, making three to ten of these at a time.

In the next session I'll create these.

And in the final session I'll load them up, schedule them in or save them to drafts. They also then get saved to the content bank to be reused later.

I've used this when designing a series of "What we do", 'FAQ' and "ABOUT US" posts. These are really important for nurturing our relationship with our followers but so easily to miss when you're busy.

One of the other benefits of this is that I can do the creation part on the days I'm feeling it most and have high levels of energy. As we've grown our business, I've been able to take days out to create, instead of using nights and weekends.

If a post does well once on social media, it's likely to do well more than once. I've had videos and posts that consistently get shares, comments and follows over and over again. It feels like cheating, but it's completely allowed.

I do know a few marketing strategists who just use content bank posts. If you've got people following you across multiple platforms, and you're repeating too often it can feel a little bit impersonal, so do make sure you're topping up the bank on a regular basis. We want a well maintained and interesting web.

CREATE YOUR OWN PLAN

As you work through this book, really take time to think about where your best customers come from and how you can invest in spending time on those platforms.

If you are just getting started, it's a good idea to use the same platforms your competitors are using at least.

Then work out a base level of content output you can maintain, keeping in mind what the minimum expected for growth in that platform is.

Block out regular times in your diary to create it, or to meet with people in your team to get it done.

EVERYTHING'S CONNECTED

The secret to keeping your head from getting overwhelmed is to learn how to repurpose your content as you spin your web.

The foundation of the content is where you spend the most time, ensuring it's in line with those key messages you created, talking to your ideal people.

Once that's created, you can take parts of that content and cut it up, put it on a different platform, reshape it, change the format, and re-spin it again and again.

If you put the hard work into the initial piece, you may only need to create several big pieces a year.

It's a big deal to write a good quality blog, create an information packed webinar, or film a video talking through a topic in depth. So if you're going to take the time and effort, it's a good idea to then maximise the use of all that energy by finding ways to repurpose that content all over the internet.

I used to use my blogs. Then I used my MAP IT Marketing podcast, I've used the content from this to create my content across everywhere else.

Now I use a system that takes my content buckets, and creates regular, targeted content ideas that attract my ideal visitors to my web. I can produce vast amounts of content because I've got structures, habits and routines in place, we've spent time creating templates and specific types of content schedules, and because I have a team who supports the creation.

Remember the black box of someone else's business?

Before you stress about how your content output compares to someone else, remember we are not playing on the same field, with the same team, or budget. I get help.

I wanted to breakdown what I'm doing to help you work out how to repurpose for your business.

I'm doing a lot more repurposing than I was doing several months ago, and I'm planning to move this up a notch again over the next six months. While it takes time, the end benefit of focussed marketing is business growth, and besides our time, and a few low-cost, paid subscriptions, it's a free marketing method.

Content marketing is about building that web of consistent messaging shared out across a range of platforms over time. Some of these may have a short lifecycle (such as an Instagram post), whereas others may have a longer catchment time (a YouTube video, a Pinterest pin, or a blog post).

IT'S OK TO DISRUPT PATTERNS

Once you start to feel comfortable with the framework and feel it's easy, you can start to modify it all.

One of my favourite things to do is to do the opposite of everyone else. It's one of the easiest ways to stick out. Plus, there are always a bunch of other people waiting for something different.

For a long time, my dream was to become a singer. I'm fair to middling good, and perhaps I could have been better, but just as in my writing, I like to take shortcuts. I love hearing the bits that are behind the melody and sing those, especially if they are easier notes to reach! The desire to sing the harmony, mixed with my dislike of memorising the words of every song made becoming a singer problematic to say the least.

In music, I love syncopation. It makes Jazz beautiful. When you sing jazz, you are meant to play in the boundaries of melody but there is an infinite number of ways you can do that. You can harmonise, riff, echo, trill, and make the sound your own playground.

I love singing the "other parts" in a song—harmony, riffs. Part of that does come down to being lazy, part of it is a drive to play and part of it is that even in a song, I'm trying to find the easiest and simplest way to stand out. I had a singing teacher once who said, "Your soul knows you need to stand out. In being different you are blending in AND standing out at the same time." and I felt seen in that moment.

While everyone else is doing the same thing... the person doing it differently—that's the person you notice. If everyone else is doing it one way and seeing success, start by copying it to learn. But if they can then start creating something outside of the norms, people notice. We scan, we scroll, we want to have something that catches our eye. We want someone or something to STAND OUT and be different.

We live in an age where our ideal clients don't want the SAME thing. They want the different thing.

So here's a question for you: As you become more confident in your writing, what patterns that you see cropping up in your feed can you BREAK every now and again?

When we disrupt by changing what we do, in a way that our target audience notices us more, we have a chance to stand out and be remembered. I'd rather be remembered by fifty ideal clients than be one of the masses for thousands.

Here's some of the ways I have mixed it up in the past:

1. Ignoring LinkedIn polls

When LinkedIn introduced polls as a post option, everyone used them. All the time. Every second post was a poll of one type or another.

I was tempted to use polls too. On the face of it, they were great for engagement. Do a poll, and you'd get a post seen by thousands.

But I also know my audience loves depth, and thinking, and insight. So I created a dummy poll, screenshotted it and then deleted the poll and used the image to talk about what I don't like about polls.

A large number of people came out and agreed, and I found more people I relate to on LinkedIn.

2. The occasional short caption

While long captions are (at the time of writing) very popular on Instagram or LinkedIn, every now and again I'll do a two- or three-line post caption instead to break up the pattern of content.

This works (for me) most if the content is light-hearted or humorous, and it's accompanied by a picture, video or reel that's self-explanatory.

3. Serious reels

While I sometimes do the "point and dance" type videos, these aren't me. I need to create content that fits with my time availability, my personality, and my goals. So most of mine are really low tech, spoken directly to camera, advice type videos.

4. Stand out brights

We went away from the earthy tones so many other female business owners were using for our branding. We also created our own templates for our content using images and fonts you can't get in canva.com to make sure our content looked different.

5. Quirky photos

Instead of getting stock standard branding photos done, to use on social media, we went with a quirkier and fun look to stand out. (However, I do regret not getting a few serious photos for those moments where quirk is not the look you are aiming for!)

You need to find your own ways of standing out. It will be different for everyone.

Being a pattern disrupter means that I may change any or all of these when they become popular, or no longer have the impact I need to be different. It's not a disruption if everyone else is doing it with you in unison!

PART EIGHT
TROUBLESHOOTING

CHAPTER 29

PERFECTIONISM

AFTER WORKING WITH THOUSANDS OF SMALL BUSINESS OWNERS, I'VE GOT A good handle on blocks, common issues and all the great excuses for NOT actioning anything from this book. We've covered most of them throughout the book but here's three more common ones.

A few years back, when we were still a "doing" agency, we worked with a business that was burning through all the marketing agencies in town. I was in love with this brand, so completely ignored all the red flags and chased them for their business.

I quickly discovered why they weren't seeing growth on social media. We used to allocate around eight hours a month to content creation for a client. This would allow for us to create and write the posts, get approval, and load them up. This would typically give them about three posts a week.

For this client, it took us the full eight hours to get ONE Instagram post approved. They wanted a full breakdown of why we'd chosen each hashtag, they asked for seventeen changes to the copy before settling on the content we'd started with, and they didn't like the images (that they had provided) and wanted something else.

Everything also had to go through final approval from the business owner, even though they had a sales and marketing team, which meant this process took over a month. You may be surprised to learn that we didn't last long as their agency either!

A perfect post is a beautiful thing. But chasing it is not going to get you growth on social media. (As an aside I checked their social media before writing this. They are posting a beautiful shot once a week to Facebook and Instagram, it's all promotional content, very little follower engagement, and they have almost the same number of followers they did five years ago. It all looks perfect. But it's sterile, and definitely not very "social".)

On my own social media accounts you're going to find typos (I'm a fast, and completely inaccurate typist, and I'm also sloppy with proofreading. I tend to notice the typo once it's live!) Sometimes a reel will post and the words suddenly go out of alignment because of a blip. Or I'll spy a slide in a carousel post with an error.

If it's early, I'll catch it and often I'll fix it. But I can tell you this—some of my most popular and growth generating posts have not been perfect. And the ones I'm most proud of, that look amazing and I poured far too much time into? All I heard were crickets when I posted them.

Now for some of you, the idea that a post may get out with a typo may be a step too far. I have a client who always alerts me when I have a typo. Sometimes I'll fix it, sometimes I won't but regardless, it drives her crazy that there's one there at all. She's very detail oriented, and used to be a proofreader for a job. To be clear, I'm not saying it's good that typos are in there, or that you need to pop them in to grow. I'm just saying, if there's one there every now and again, it's going to be ok.

If we're focusing on serving our audience instead of ourselves, we stop (hopefully) trying to cover ourselves with a facade of perfection, and show the real side a little more.

ALWAYS SOMEONE BETTER THAN YOU (AND ALWAYS SOMEONE WORSE)

There would have been a time where I would have won the gold medal for the most anxiety induced from comparisonitis.

I used to get completely paralysed when seeing others in my industry do better than me and see success I wasn't seeing. And of course, now I know about how every business is a black box, and we're all on different journeys, and perhaps this platform is the only one they have, but I've got more going on somewhere different, and they've got a full-time marketing manager, and I don't, but back then I didn't know that.

Of course, I wasn't looking at all the people who were worse than me for, you know, balance!

There is always going to be someone who is doing things better than you. And there's always going to be someone who's not quite where you are yet.

My rule of thumb, when following accounts who are doing better than me is to stick with the ones that inspire me, and unfollow everyone else. Lifes too short to walk around with feelings of inadequacy!

Focus on your audience, not your competitors.

CHAPTER 30

A LACK OF TIME

IT TAKES TIME, EFFORT AND FOCUS TO BUILD YOUR CAPTURE SPIRAL. IT doesn't matter how fast you create it, as long as you create at a steady pace.

In terms of weekly commitment, you will need to allocate regular time.

"How much time will this take?" has to be one of the most common questions I get asked about marketing. I have a general formula, that's calculated on the size of your team. For every full-time employee you have (if you're a solopreneur that's you) you should budget four hours a week to marketing, plus add in a day every four to six weeks to help plan, prepare and create your content, and check everything's going to plan.

If you've got the equivalent of five full-time employees, that's twenty hours a week. It's a general guide to help you remember to "feed" the web, so that you get enough people making their way to the Hub and working with you on a consistent basis.

Of course, you can do more, and if you are a new business, you may need to. If we are launching a course, creating a new offer, or growing a new area of our business, the initial time in ensuring everything is set up takes more than our usual time budget.

It also often feels painful to fit in, as we still have to "do" our normal work.

When someone complains about the time, I often ask how much time they tend to spend in the sales process. Often you'll find, especially with service-based businesses, that the sales process is vastly shortened if your web is strong, effective and super sticky. It does all the hard work for you.

We've gone from having to have two to three in person meetings, to often only needing one short sales meeting via Zoom. Sometimes the person we're meeting has already committed via email, and it's just us working out the details. That's what building a web does.

It's the same for product-based businesses. A strong web where you've built a community means selling becomes simple. All you've got to do is share your excitement, and the wallets come out.

While some people are pleasantly surprised at the amount of time, others feel it's far too much time to put aside for marketing. If you've traditionally done well with good word of mouth and repeat business, it can feel like a waste of time to invest the time in marketing.

CAN YOU SURVIVE THE LULL?

We often get asked how long it will take to see results from building a web.

Of course, I'm itching to say "it depends" because of course it does depend! If you've already got a good list of existing clients, you've already built a web, and it just needs tweaking, and your business is healthy, the results can be fast, dramatic and exciting.

Alternatively, if you've fallen into a cycle of needing to get a certain number of sales every day to just survive, struggling to pay yourself, struggling to find your sweet spot, and are going to need to completely overhaul everything, or you're starting from scratch, the answer will be different.

We're all at different stages in our journey. The results will always be different. If you decided to read all of this book, do all the work and apply it, and keep at it consistently for six weeks you'd see results of people moving closer. They might not quite be at the Hub, ready to buy, but you'd expect them to start to connect and accept your offer to nurture that relationship a bit further. They'd be happy members of your sticky web.

It will be longer if you're trying to put out fires in other areas of your business. We've had a few clients whose businesses are so broken in terms of a "pay to play" cycle of using expensive ads, along with a sales cycle that's very dependent on one-to-one sales, with numerous meetings, who have been unable to pay the short-term price of a slight drop in revenue as they've adjusted their schedules, and started to prioritise marketing.

AIM FOR THE RUSH YOU GET WHEN A SALE COMES IN

It's pretty unmotivating to be showing up, putting your face out in public, putting in the effort and not getting the 'ching ching' of great leads and sales. Six weeks is a short amount of time when you look back five years later. But during those six weeks? Every day is one more you could just go get a quick fix the old way.

If you believe you can't survive the possible drop of sales that could happen while you build your web, either commit to build it super slowly over time, or spend some time working out how to fix your business, and reduce the cost that's causing you to need that constant feeding of the machine.

WHEN YOU ARE TOO BUSY

When we have someone approach us to work on a marketing strategy, we now talk about what capacity they'll likely need to set aside for marketing. Generally being too busy to fit marketing in is either a pricing issue (you aren't making enough profit to give yourself time to work on your business), a systems issue (you're unable to work efficiently enough to get the work done) or a resource issue (you don't have enough people doing the work).

If it's not any of these things, it's an attitude problem. Yes, I'm going for the jugular!

You say you want to do more marketing because you know you should, but really, it's the same as me wanting to run a marathon, and never quite getting out of bed in the morning to go for a training run. The heffalump still needs to run.

We need to take time to build up habits, create structure and sometimes get extra help to make sure the capture spiral continues to be weaved, no matter how busy we are, or how much we feel like making it happen. There is no "one activity" you do that makes it all work except HABIT.

Sometimes there are a lot of skills to learn. This is why I recommend building your web with as few radius lines as possible, and build your capture spiral using these. Slowly add more radius lines in as you develop fluency in your starter platforms. It is completely ok to go at the pace you learn, slowly add in activity over time and get the habits made.

Even a simple plan can still be overwhelming, unless you take the time you need to adopt it. Sometimes you don't often even need ALL of the plan to get you there. I've got a very long list of things I WANT to do or try for Identify. Sometimes you can't do it all. And that's ok.

CHAPTER 31

CONSISTENCY

CONSISTENCY IS BETTER THAN SPORADIC EXCELLENCE

WHATEVER YOU DECIDE TO DO, MAKE IT CONSISTENT. IF THAT IS YOU committing to posting on a platform twice a week and you can maintain it, then that's far better than posting twice a day for a week and then ghosting the platform.

I often say social media is like a kitten. It needs feeding often and loves attention. You can't just opt out of feeding that cat for a week because you spent too much time feeding it last week! (Or for all of us ancients —it's a little like those tamagotchis you had to keep alive!)

Over time, the level of consistency might change, and as you become more confident that it's all working, you may add in some extra posts and pour in energy.

Committing to consistency is committing to accepting that not every post will be perfect, or gold standard. The goal is to aim for about eighty percent of your best work, consistently. I'm not asking you to be crappy. I'm just asking you to balance this with the rest of your business, and make it happen.

This allows us to accept the odd imperfection, trust our audience, and allow for that random post you put together in three minutes to go viral because it was odd enough to attract attention at just the right moment.

CONSISTENTLY BAD IS NOT THE GOAL

When we first start something, adding the routine into our schedule might be the first goal. Showing up is enough, even if you're not using the best images, or writing anything compelling.

While it's a good idea to school yourself on how to structure a post, or what you need to say, or why you're there in the first place (hint: that's what this book should have helped you with!), it's often not until you're doing it all in a live test that you can see if it's all going to work for you.

Once you've got the habit sorted, you can just stick to what you are doing, or you can commit yourself to small improvements. And when I say you "can commit" what I'm really saying is "please do commit!"

There needs to be an ongoing wave of moving from "this all feels easy and I'm in a good routine" to "I'm learning new skills and this feels uncomfortable". If you want to stay on top of how best to serve your audience online. Each platform has an algorithm that's an amalgamation of what all the people on that platform are watching, reading and interacting with.

The type of content, the way it's delivered, the amount of captions, the images, everything changes overtime. Our accounts aren't meant to look and sound the same year in, year out. They are meant to evolve, and follow the customer's behaviour.

Consistency is a huge part of success when it comes to social media. But continuous improvement needs to also play a part.

WHEN YOU NEED TO TAKE A BREAK

Last year I consciously took a few weeks break off from TikTok. I was feeling overwhelmed, confused and I needed to work out what I was actually there for.

If you are in a slump and nothing's working, taking a break is ok. I also often take a break over the summer period too, but that's more about cocktails and swimming!

I would suggest, if you've got an engaged following, that you do pop up a post saying you're AWOL but coming back. Otherwise, just disappear for a bit, and take the time to get your head clear.

I did this ten years ago on Twitter, came back after two weeks and quickly realised it was no longer the right platform for me at that time, and took the app from my phone. Since then I've pretty much just used it for link sharing. This may change in the future, but right now it's the right fit.

When I took time off TikTok, I realised I needed some more time to work out what I wanted to do there, and it was a strategy issue. So I created some content that helped me tread water on the app, scheduled it in, and then took more time to look at my overall strategy.

Going back to TikTok after that time, I saw my account grow faster, and engagement shoot up. I've done the same on Instagram and LinkedIn, with similar results.

Taking thoughtful breaks every now and again can help you reset. However, all the platforms thrive best with consistency, so take breaks sporadically, with purpose, and accept that it might take a while for you to recoup the momentum you had prior to the break.

The other reason a break can be a good thing is if you're got mental health struggles that are making social media an unsafe place for you right now. That's a good sign to pull back from time online, and take more time in the "real world".

If you're needing to do this on a regular basis, or have work that has big periods of business that makes content creation hard to juggle, having a clear content calendar and scheduling posts in advance can help you stay consistent through it all.

PART NINE
OVER TO YOU NOW

CHAPTER 32
PUTTING IT ALL TOGETHER

ONE OF MY BAD HABITS HALFWAY THROUGH A BOOK IS TO DECIDE I'VE figured it out and just find that book's version of this chapter. If that's what you have done, hello there friend! I see you!

Often, of course, I find I've missed an essential detail and have to go back to reading the book. But here's to those of us who always aim for the shortcuts in life first!

For the rest of you, who gainfully worked your way through this book from start to finish, we're at the finish line! Here's where we are going to bring all your actions together. This is your time to weave your own content web, your way.

Remember to download all the worksheets and guides from **beaspiderbuildaweb.com** to help put this all together.

TIME TO BUILD YOUR WEB

Before we start to create your web, we need to make sure we know where we are going to build it and why.

BE A KIND SPIDER

If you follow everything in this book, and don't start with seeing yourself as a kind spider, none of it will work. Sure, you'll get some wins from creating a sticky web. You'll catch people and you'll be able to convince them to work with you.

We want to build a web that people love being on. We want them to feel safe about inviting their friends. We want them to come back to the Decision Hub every time they need what we sell.

To do that we need to start with a kind spider attitude.

This involves trusting the process. It means being patient and knowing that it's going to work.

This is a brave step. It feels completely counterintuitive. It's scary to weave something, and know you are trusting the people who are attracted to it, to make their own way to you. But if you don't, your spider's web is going to feel strange to anyone who visits it. It won't feel like a safe play to stay. This is your first job.

Remember you are a kind spider.

You are also a unique spider. No one else does things exactly the way you do. No one has had exactly the same life experiences, understanding or knowledge you have. Your way of doing things will always be different to your competitors. This is how you stand out.

Our job is to help the visitors to our web trust us. One of the fastest ways to do that is to show ourselves. It's not compulsory. I'm still going to encourage you to do it.

You are a unique spider. And you have never killed a man with your face.

DEFINE YOUR ANCHOR POINT

No matter how beautiful your web is, if it's not created with a strong anchor point, it's always going to be a fragile one.

Building a sticky web takes a lot of effort and time. We want to make it one that can weather changes, be able to be renovated here and there, but does not have to be made from scratch over and over again.

Taking time to define your business values, and what you stand for is key before you start to weave your web. Take time to work through the process outlined in Part Two, and make sure your values are ones you can live by today. (Values are not aspirational.)

Our values are the anchor of our web.

It's a good idea to also look at your own capacity, and where you are sitting in terms of business, life and your time. Marketing overwhelm can cripple any ability to build an effective web. It's better to build slowly and consistently, than trying to get it all up, designed and ready within a few weeks. A sticky web takes time to build.

NARROW YOUR ARROW

To make it possible to weave our web along multiple radius lines with sticky content, we need to narrow the arrow of who we are going to talk to, what we will offer them and what we are going to talk about.

If you're still fuzzy on any of these three, go back and work through Part Three. The combination of our target market, our core offers and our narrow messages makes our weaving consistent. It helps us design our Decision Hub, choose our radius lines, and create our content bank when we weave our capture spiral.

My personality always craves to jump to the fun stuff. The creative parts. I have had to make myself work in these areas. For a long time, I tried to just go with my gut. As a reformed gut marketer, I can promise you that taking the time to work through these three steps will provide you with far more people knocking on the door of your Decision Hub.

Take the time and narrow your arrow.

BUILD THE TRUST BRIDGE

If you're an existing business, you have some work to do before you build your sticky web. You need to check you are already getting repeat customers, and word of mouth referrals. If you aren't you need to take time to build an effective trust bridge.

If you try to skip over this part, your web will be weak. Every time a little gust of the unexpected turns up, your web will shake off everyone who's on it, even if they're trying to hang on for dear life. We need the stability of trust to build a secure web.

In Part Four I told you the tale of how we once broke the trust bridge, and the effort it took to rebuild it. The effort to grow a business with a strong trust bridge is much easier. The more you strengthen the trust bridge, the easier it is for customers to come back to the Decision Hub over and over again. They also bring their friends and contacts. The trust bridge saves you time, money and effort as you grow your business.

If you are a new business, create good customer service processes to build your trust bridge right from the start. It will keep your sticky web strong, protect it in times of stress, and help you create a beautiful sticky web.

CREATE YOUR DECISION HUB

While a Decision Hub can be your office, a retail store or an event, our sticky web focus was on creating a website to help people make contact, become a lead or even purchase from you.

Part Five walked you through the must-haves of a converting website, helping you make it easy for people to make the decision to buy from you.

Some business owners spend a lot of time building their web on social media platforms they don't own, without the Decision Hub of their own website to capture information, and help bring people to the stickiest parts of your web.

Your website will help you build trust, remove objections, and most of all, make it very easy to buy from you. This is the next step in building your web.

THE DECISION HUB DOOR

We want the relationships we build on our web to last. Sometimes people will come close to buying, then bounce back up the web. Others will walk on through those doors, buy from you then go back out and hang out on the web, ready to come see you again another time.

Along with creating content for them on the social media platforms you've chosen as your radius lines, you can build a long-term relationship with these Decision Door visitors with email.

To build a web that provides the most sales with the least amount of effort, make sure you add the radius of email.

SELECT YOUR RADIUS LINES

Our radius lines are where we will spin our capture spiral and lay down all of our content. One of these is a given, our website. Another should be your emails. The rest will depend on your narrow arrow target, offer and messages. They may also depend on your time, skill level, and level of commitment. Some radius lines take longer to build out than others.

While one business may have nine radius lines, you may only start with three. Someone else may have five. You need to make the decision for yourself of which ones fit you best. In Part Six we look at how to choose the best ones for your business, and why I can't make that choice for you in this book.

IT'S TIME TO CAPTURE PEOPLE!

Once we've selected our anchor point, built our trust bridge, and found our Decision Hub, spinning out radius lines out to the edges, we're ready to build our capture spiral.

I've already mentioned my impulsive desire to take action. I find this part of building a web the hardest part of all. I want to read a little, then jump in and take action. Last year I focused myself to sit down and plan out our marketing using the same structure I've given you in the book.

It took every ounce of effort to not jump up and start creating before I was done. I made myself do exactly what I'm asking you to do. Sit down and work through the process in Part Seven. Create your content bank and take time to work out how best to talk to people from the outside edges of Noticed to the slightly sticky Interested, to the sticky Nurtured right through to the super-stuck-with-all-the-stickies Yours.

Take the time to get this right and weaving the capture spiral becomes easy. You know what you need to say, when you need to say it, and why it's going to work.

Use the worksheets provided on **beaspiderbuildaweb.com** to help build out a capture spiral that will bring them right to your door.

HERE'S HOW I CAN HELP

Right at the beginning I said I didn't want to waste your time. So, all I'm going to ask you to do is take action on at least one concept from this book and apply it to your business. If you do that and stick to it, the time you spent on this book will have been worth it.

For those who like to plan more than taking action, remember to push yourself a little before you are ready to act.

For those of you who love taking action, remember to spend time planning a little.

Make sure you download all the worksheets from **beaspiderbuildaweb.com** and use them to help your business. You'll have to give me your email to download everything. I want to promise you I'm going to honour that email. I'm not planning to send you weeks of long emails. I promise. But I'd like to stay in touch. I'd like to hear about your business and what you're doing.

When you ask for the worksheets, I'll send them to you on the email address you've provided. We'll also send you a link to our MAP IT Marketing Facebook group, where you can ask questions and mix with other business owners. You can use the free training there to help you with your radius lines and capture spirals.

I'll also send you links to my podcast, YouTube, and social links so you can come be a part of my web if you like. Please come and say hi, and let me know what you thought of the book!

I hope you're feeling excited about how you can be a kind spider for your business. I can't wait to hear about the web you're weaving.

May it be beautiful and extra sticky.

Rachel

ABOUT THE AUTHOR

After collecting different careers like butterflies, Rachel Klaver discovered they all led to marketing.

For more than ten years she's worked with small business owners on their marketing, with a specific interest in content marketing strategy.

As a small business owner often low on time, and a distinct aversion to admin, Rachel loves helping other small businesses catch the marketing bug, with her weekly podcast MAP IT Marketing, her weekly column in *Stuff* and her content on any platform they let her have an account!

facebook.com/groups/mapitwithrachelklaver
instagram.com/identifymarketing

THANK YOU

It's a lot easier to write a book when you're a full-time writer, have young children, work completely from home and are single. While I confess to the occasional 3 a.m. start for some peace and quiet, I had to write this book in short bursts over months, instead of my previous style of writing it over two weeks, with little sleep and a meal plan of "everyone gets baked beans for dinner again!"

Thank you to our clients and the MAP IT community on Facebook who have cheered me on and helped me have so many great stories and insights. Your encouragement and belief in me pushed me to the finish line!

Thank you to my three children whose cleverness and creativity inspire me every day. Being your Ma helped me find my voice, discover what I love and learn that passion isn't enough if you need to feed your kids more than two-minute noodles!

I couldn't have done this book without the company of Spud, George and Milly. Dogs have to be the best for writer's block cuddles.

And to Rod. Your support both as a husband and as a business partner is valued every day. I know I'm a pain when my brain is noisy in the mornings and I can't talk, when I need to start work at 3 a.m. when I'm melting down because I booked too many client calls, and I didn't get my writing fix, and when I say I'm going to do it all over again next year. Couldn't do it without you.

NOTES

3. YOU ARE A UNIQUE SPIDER

1. A Heffalump is a type of elephant-like character in the Winnie the Pooh stories by A. A. Milne

9. YOU NEED TO NARROW YOUR ARROW

1. Clubhouse is a social media platform that is pure live audio. You can join a room, listen to the speakers and contribute to the discussion. It started as an invite only to IPhone users creating a steady stream of posts asking if "anyone had an invite to give" It was immensely popular in the earlier parts of 2021, then America went back to work after lockdowns, summer came, and the people disappeared.

12. A MASERATI FOR $4.99

1. Natalie Coombe, a pricing expert, helped me work through a list of barriers that business owners can have around money for this chapter. (You can check her work out at www.nataliecoombe.com).

21. SHOWING THEM THE LOVE

1. *I was completely OBSESSED with trapdoor spiders as a kid. And petrified of them. That and sinking sand. It's actually incredible that I still love the beach so much.*

26. THE STEPS TO CREATING THE CONTENT FOR YOUR CAPTURE SPIRAL

1. Kate Toon is a marketer based in Australia. She's best known for her SEO and Copywriting courses and is an exemplary digital marketer with her own distinct style.